Praise for
The 8 Laws of Customer-Focused Leadership

"If every leader 'knows' customer performance is essential, then why are so many companies bad at it or at best mediocre? Blake's book does a great job providing content, not just stories, on how to improve. It applies to every company, not just consumer brands." —DAVID COTE, former CEO of Honeywell and author of *Winning Now, Winning Later*

"As customers evolve from boomers to Gen Z and those beyond, 'customers' are changing rapidly. Work-from-home, dislocation, and societal forces have reshaped everything from hiring to culture building. Leadership today is a new game. Blake's eight laws are destined to become a reference guide for leaders in this new day and age." —SHAWN D. NELSON, founder and CEO, Lovesac

"If you're a leader seeking to make customer satisfaction a top priority, this book is your ultimate guide. Blake's framework is a treasure trove of wisdom that will help you create a culture that truly cares about the customer." —DORIE CLARK, *Wall Street Journal* bestselling author of *The Long Game* and executive education faculty, Columbia Business School

"If you want your customers to feel connected to you and to know that you place them at the center of your decisions, *The 8 Laws of Customer-Focused Leadership* is a valuable playbook. After studying the most esteemed companies and interviewing thousands of executives, Blake has distilled the essential steps to build a business and brand that customers love." —EDUARDO BRICEÑO, author of *The Performance Paradox*

"To achieve an exceptional customer experience, leadership is the cornerstone. Blake has crafted an inspirational and practical guide for those who are, or aspire to be, leaders in customer experience. Recognizing that your customer is the primary source of value for your business, this book serves as a powerful motivator to maintain focus on this critical priority." —STEVEN VAN BELLEGHEM, author of *A Diamond in the Rough* and CX inspirator

"An incredible customer experience is your key to rapid growth and business success. In this book, Blake lays out the essentials of delivering a world-class customer experience in a simple-to-understand manner." —ALLAN DIB, bestselling author of *The 1-Page Marketing Plan* and *Lean Marketing*

"Customer experience isn't an initiative—it's a way of life. The most successful businesses in the world pair an ethic of customer experience with systems and processes that allow them to deliver remarkable interactions on a consistent basis. If you want a customer-focused organization, Blake can show you the way."

—JOEY COLEMAN, international keynote speaker
and *Wall Street Journal* bestselling author of
Never Lose a Customer Again and *Never Lose an Employee Again*

"Blake's new book serves as a compass for leaders at all levels, guiding us toward creating unforgettable customer experiences through empathy, innovation, and strategic foresight."
—DONNA MORRIS,
chief people officer, Walmart

"Although Build-A-Bear is largely known as customer-focused, it still requires consistent reinforcement across the entire organization to assure we keep our guests at the center of our value proposition. Blake's key insights, real life examples, and clear presentation of the eight laws provide a practical approach aligned with many of the core tenets that have proven useful for our company's overall success."
—SHARON PRICE JOHN,
president and CEO, Build-A-Bear Workshop

"No company can afford to rest on its laurels—Blake's smart, measured predictions are the keys to staying relevant and profitable in an ever-shifting business landscape. While change is always in the air, the central tenet of this book—that the customer experience must always come first—will never go out of style."
—CHEF ROBERT IRVINE,
author of *Overcoming Impossible*

"In this book, Blake does an extraordinary job of clearly outlining how imperative it is for leaders to be obsessed with serving their customers. Her eight laws will help any leader and company become a more loved brand." —TRICIA GRIFFITH,
president and CEO, Progressive Insurance

"This book is a must-read for leaders who want to transform their organizations into customer-centric powerhouses. Blake's framework is not just a blueprint; it's a masterclass in fostering a culture that revolves around exceeding customer expectations."
—OSCAR MUNOZ,
former CEO and chairman, United Airlines

"There is no shortage of companies that espouse the principles of customer centricity, but few live and breathe them to the extent that drives powerful outcomes across their entire business. The eight laws lay out a clear case that not only can strong financial outcomes coexist successfully with customer focus; they can accelerate with them."
—DARREN MacDONALD,
chief customer officer, Petco

BLAKE MORGAN

The
Laws

of Customer-Focused
Leadership

New Rules for Building a Business
Around Today's Customer

HarperCollins
Leadership

An Imprint of HarperCollins

ISBN 978-1-4002-4596-3 (eBook)

ISBN 978-1-4002-4595-6 (HC)

Library of Congress Cataloging-in-Publication Data
Library of Congress Cataloging-in-Publication application has been submitted.

Printed in the United States of America

24 25 26 27 28 LBC 5 4 3 2 1

This book is dedicated to Jacob Morgan,
my untiring advocate, my rock, and the loving father
to our two wonderful children, Naomi and Noah.

Contents

Contents

Customer experience is the best
marketing money can't buy.

You may have never heard of Mel Fisher, but he was one of the greatest treasure hunters who ever lived. He was born on a chicken farm in 1922 and grew up loving stories about pirates and divers. Mel fought in World War II on the beaches of Normandy. After the war, he returned to the US and opened a dive shop in Los Angeles. He married Dolores Horton in 1953, and together they had five children.

In 1969, a customer told Mel about a Spanish shipwreck called *Nuestra Señora de Atocha* that sank from a hurricane in 1622. It sat at the bottom of the ocean off the coast of Key West, Florida. Mel decided to close his diving shop and move to Key West in search of this sunken treasure.

When he got to Florida, Mel invented his own diving equipment to scour the bottom of the ocean. After two years, he got the first sign that he was on the right track when he found a single lead musket ball from the ship. Little did he know that his search would not be over for many years. Mel kept up his contagious enthusiasm and energy for years, going out every day in search of treasure.

As his children grew up, Mel enlisted their help in searching for the *Atocha*. One fateful day, his eldest son's ship capsized, killing his son, his son's wife, and another diver. While he was very upset, he continued his focus. He had a contagiously positive spirit and was undeterred even in the face of tragedy. Every day, Mel would say, "Today is the day!"—he had an unwavering belief that he would eventually find the shipwreck he dreamed about.

It took sixteen years of hunting before Mel and his family found the main shipwreck of the *Atocha* in 1985. The treasure they discovered was worth $450 million! Mel's dream became a reality. He was triumphant.

But Mel's journey didn't end there. He and the family had to fight the state of Florida for eight years over who owned the treasure. The case went all the way up to the Supreme Court, where it was decided that Mel Fisher would get to keep his treasure. One day I was telling this story in a keynote speech to a group of accountants and they told me afterward that their firm did Mel Fisher's taxes in the '80s. Mel was a legend because he would give the accountants coins as gifts.

RELENTLESS

Mel Fisher is described as relentless because he never gave up on his dream, even when others couldn't see his vision. It's not just about energy and enthusiasm or the faith that you will ultimately reach your goals if you put in the work. For people like Mel Fisher it was putting in the work every day, even in the darkest of circumstances.

Another charismatic innovator jumped out of bed in the morning with enthusiasm for many years without pay. He was also looking for treasure and used his vision and military mindset to achieve his goals.

Jeff Bezos struggled for many years before Amazon became the behemoth it is today. In fact, he loved hard work so much that he intended to call Amazon "Relentless.com" and bought the URL in 1994. If you go to Relentless.com today, it redirects to Amazon.com. In his own way, Jeff Bezos is very similar to Mel Fisher. Both were called crazy by many people who couldn't see their genius or appreciate their tenacity for something that wasn't obvious at first sight.

In the early days, Bezos was known for saying, "I think our company is undervalued. . . . The world just doesn't understand what Amazon is going to be." As Bezos created more products and grew his companies, he continued his relentless approach. He gave Blue Origin a coat of arms and a Latin motto, *Gradatim ferociter*, which translates to "Step by Step, Ferociously." He set an example for his teams who believed in him and made his dream a reality.

We all want to find treasure like Mel Fisher. We want to hit the jackpot like Jeff Bezos.

The treasure chest that great leaders seek today is a customer focus that leads to unimaginable treasure—strong relationships, loyal customers, innovation, engagement, and, yes, better revenue. Finding that treasure requires taking an enthusiastic journey toward customer-centric leadership with a total focus on customer experience. In many ways, it goes against traditional ideas of what it means to be a leader or concepts learned in business school.

The path to a customer-centric company is paved with leadership. A leader is nothing without a group of followers—but a leader is granted that title because other people *choose* to follow them. If the employees do not trust or respect the leader, they are simply a manager. And without trusting employees, you cannot build a customer-centric company.

In this book I will provide the map, coordinates, and key to your very own treasure chest.

By knowing the rules of customer-focused leadership, working on them in yourself, and setting an example to impart them to others, you will transform yourself into the kind of leader organizations need the most right now. A customer experience mindset is something leaders must develop.

Now let's move to a discussion on how a relentless focus on the customer has become the key competitive advantage for organizations today.

1

The Rise of the Customer-Focused Leader

Customer experience boiled down into a very simple concept is this: it's cool to care! Remember so many movies in the '90s and early 2000s about not caring about work? How about the movie *Office Space*, or the show *The Office*. What has become very clear is that today's companies that care are actually winning. And the companies that do not care—they are not in a hurry to maintain relevance—disappear quickly. They think that the world doesn't notice their apathy, but today the cream rises to the top. Today good and bad news travels back, and the world is too busy to spend money with companies that are not grateful for the work.

This is not a book about transactions; this is a book about how to live. If most of your life is work, showing up at work every day and caring about your work is very important. Think about companies like RadioShack, BlackBerry, Sears, Blockbuster, Mervyn's, Pan Am, Palm (Pilot), Borders, and WorldCom. These companies dissolved because—very simply put—they got confused about what mattered. Customer experience is not just a concept we're going to talk about today; it's a way of life. Customer experience is the act of caring about your work, taking pride in your work, and not letting nonsense run or ruin your company. Who knew that getting your priorities straight and reducing back-end complexity could be the coolest thing you could do as a leader! Customer experience is many things: it's innovation, it's your people, it's your culture, it's your ethics, it's how you make money, it's your suppliers, it's your politics, it's everything. But let's laser in a little more, and get specific.

Customer experience is the perception the customer has of your brand. But the customer experience doesn't include only the transaction of the customer buying the product from you—it starts with the initial awareness that your brand exists. How do they discover you and what do they see, hear, or experience? The experience is also how the customer decides whether or not to buy the product or service. Then comes the actual experience of the customer buying the product from you. Customer service is an important but often overlooked piece of it. Customer loyalty and advocacy programs, including how often customers buy from you, refer others or talk about you in a negative or positive way. I believe customer experience = business, and you cannot have one without the other. You simply cannot have a business without your customers.

Part of my job as a customer experience futurist is to look at the horizon and translate what I see for the business world.

And while I'm a futurist looking forward, I also look back to see how we got here. To understand the future, a futurist must also study the past.

Over the past ten years, we've seen an explosion of businesses caring about customers. Corporate employee titles with the word *customer* exploded worldwide.[1] In 2016, a McKinsey study showed only 39 percent of organizations had a customer-centric role. In 2017, 65 percent of companies[2] had a chief customer or chief experience officer; by 2020, that number jumped to 90 percent of companies. Today, a search on LinkedIn generates ninety-four hundred titles of chief customer officer.

What changed?

Simply put, technology drove this new era of accountability and focus on the customer.

Companies used to have all the power. But by the mid-2000s—with the proliferation of social media and smartphones—that changed quickly. Luckily customer relationship management technology improved, allowing companies to better track who their customers were, where they had been, and what they might need in the future. I had the chance to teach at the Rutgers Executive MBA Program on how to build a "customer experience technology stack"—and that is something that did not exist just a few years ago.

Start-ups like Zappos got a lot of attention for being some of the first companies to treat customers like royalty and get away from the *cost*-centric mentalities and metrics traditionally held by the contact center. With visionary leaders like Tony Hsieh, these companies actually loved their customers. After the rise of social media around 2006, employees and customers felt empowered to tell the world about their experiences, and companies had little power to do anything.

Over the years, innovation and technology made all kinds of experiences much better. The early decades of the 2000s witnessed several groundbreaking innovations and experiences across various fields. There is no denying that advances in technology affected every walk of life—especially customer experience. But you can't look at what is happening in customer experience in a vacuum without looking at all the other places consumers are getting incredible customer experiences.

Innovations from the Early Twenty-First Century

- **Smartphones and mobile apps:** The iPhone debuted in 2007 and revolutionized personal technology. Mobile apps transformed the way people communicate, work, shop, and entertain themselves. Very rarely does anyone hail a taxi anymore.

- **Social media:** Facebook, founded in 2004, and Twitter, founded in 2006, changed how people connect, share information, and express themselves online. Customer experiences were now recorded on phones and replayed for the world to see and judge—for better or worse.

- **Virtual worlds and gaming:** Massively multiplayer online role-playing games like *World of Warcraft* (released in 2004) created immersive online experiences, connecting millions of players worldwide.

- **E-commerce:** Amazon and eBay expanded e-commerce, making it easier for people to shop online. Amazon introduced innovations like Amazon Prime, which changed the way people think about online shopping and delivery. Even today Amazon is testing delivery by drone in one hour or less in London to deliver medications.[3]

- **Streaming services:** The '00s saw the rise of streaming platforms like Netflix (streaming launched in 2007) and YouTube. These services disrupted traditional TV and movie distribution.

- **Google Earth:** Google Earth, launched in 2005, provided a new way to explore the world through satellite imagery. It was a pioneering experience in geospatial visualization.

- **Crowdsourcing and open source:** The '00s saw the emergence of collaborative platforms like Wikipedia and open-source software development, where communities of volunteers contributed to knowledge and technology.

- **Space tourism:** The early decades of the '00s saw the emergence of space tourism ventures like Virgin Galactic and SpaceX, offering the possibility of civilian space travel.

- **Electric and hybrid vehicles:** Companies like Tesla began producing electric vehicles, sparking interest in sustainable transportation and innovative battery technology. Teslas were very beautiful, arguably the most beautiful car run on a battery at that time.

- **AI advancements:** The early twenty-first century witnessed breakthroughs in artificial intelligence, with innovations like IBM's Watson winning at *Jeopardy!* in 2011 and the rise of deep learning techniques. Open.ai and ChatGPT are now creating conversations all over the world about how industries will be affected.

On this previous list, social media and smartphones were one of the biggest trends affecting customer experience. As customers, we all have a great amount of power because we have access to an incredible amount of information. There's no hiding. Today, we know what is happening everywhere, and we know quickly. We're all watching one another all the time. Employers are watching employees, employees are watching employers, employees are watching customers, and customers are watching employees and employers.

With all that watching, we've entered a new period of extreme accountability.

Whether you like it or not, we are all accountable to the customer. The customer has the power. Your product or service is a commodity; if it hasn't become one yet, it's only a matter of time. Even if you have a new product idea, someone will come along and make it better or different and sell more than you (see figure 1-1).

Disrupted Brands

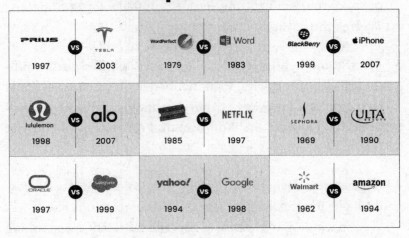

FIGURE 1-1

THE CUSTOMER EXPERIENCE ADVANTAGE

Today, the only way to differentiate your brand is through customer experience. If there are hundreds of every type of product or service, what makes customers remember you and want to return? Customer loyalty died during COVID when customers no longer had the luxury of doing business with the companies they had up to that point. Customers had to focus on surviving, and the companies that made their lives easier won their business.

Think of the brands that everyone loves—the brands people will wait in line to engage with, brands like Amazon, Nike, Starbucks, Apple, Costco, Spotify, Netflix, Louis Vuitton, Delta, Lululemon, American Express, Charles Schwab, Visa, Trader Joe's, Toyota, Warby Parker, USAA, Safelite, Discount Tire, Sephora, and T-Mobile. These brands—including the touring pop stars—all started with an objective: each saw a gap in the marketplace and wanted an experience-led brand. I drive a Hybrid Toyota Highlander. My car was in the shop, but they forgot to service one part. They then called me back to tell me, and instead of charging me for the service, they did it for free and offered to tint my windows at no cost. This is why I bought a Toyota without test-driving any other cars—I knew I could count on them, and if something went wrong they would fix it. The brand promise is the best marketing collateral you could ever use to entice a customer.

It's kind of like looking for a life partner—everyone gets along when life is easy, but what about when the wheels accidentally fall off. When everything is good and easy, everyone shows up, but how about when things go wrong? How brands show up for customers in the worst of times is what their reputation will be.

Beloved brands understand that it's not just about curating a nice selection of groceries, building a smartphone, selling a bag, creating a music app, or getting fans to a concert. To become a beloved brand you must live and breathe customer experience and interpret what that means for your company because no two are alike.

Customer experience requires a mastery of the basics. But it's more than that. Great customer experience is created when it is part of your brand. In fact, customer experience is the brand. Consider Louis Vuitton, in the words of podcast hosts Ben Gilbert and David Rosenthal of the popular technology podcast *Acquired*. One episode details the history of LVMH, and how French founder Bernard Arnault turned a $15 million investment in a bankrupt French textile company into the world's largest individual fortune. No one thought he would be capable of taking this company and building a luxury group of companies, but Arnault was a customer experience futurist, and still is, making him the (currently) second richest person in the world. Louis Vuitton's bag on its own holds value because it's a quality-made product, but carrying that bag means enough to people that they are willing to pay a premium for it. According to these podcasters it all works into the strategy.

If you think about what you're doing when you're selling luxury, you are selling the experience.

You're not selling a piece of leather. You're selling a dream.
—DAVID ROSENTHAL

David Rosenthal said, "You're not selling a piece of leather. You're selling a dream. . . . [The customer is] buying into the Louis Vuitton dream, incorporating a little bit of that dream into their life, and identifying themselves with this token, so you need to provide the best possible way for them to do that."

IF THE BRAND is the experience, the product itself isn't the only matter of importance. The complete experience around the product, the psychology of the customer—their perception about the idea of your brand—matters a great deal.

The leader must ask themselves, "How can I do what is best for employees but also for customers too?" If you make a decision that's good for customers but bad for employees, that is going to affect the culture. The experience around the product is just as important as the product itself, but your entire company must collaborate to build that experience. The product is also the experience of working at your company—and that is what your culture is. For LVMH, the luxury of the customer experience is in the fabric of the company. There's no other feeling like being on the LVMH website or in the store. LVMH understands the psychology of luxury, that it's not totally rational; it's emotional, it's psychological.

So how do you create this customer-centric culture? As a leader, it starts with you. You can't force employees to jump out of bed in the morning saying, "Today is the day I get to serve customers," or "I get to solve really hard problems!" You can inspire greatness in employees only by modeling the behavior and setting the ground-work to drive the behaviors that lead to customer-focused out-comes. You can work to reduce back-end complexity so employees are free to focus on their roles and not the messiness of a poorly run company.

Additionally in the last ten years more research has surfaced about the profound impact employee experience has on customer experience. According to a recent *Harvard Business Review* Analytic Services survey, 55 percent of executives surveyed said they believe it is just not possible to provide a great customer experience with-out providing a great employee experience.[4]

It's like Marriott founder J. W. Marriott once said: "Take care of your associates and they'll take care of your customers." Customer-centric organizations have employees who are 60 percent more engaged. Investing in employee experience can generate a high ROI for the organization.

Google searches on the phrase "employee experience" have grown exponentially. Figure 1-2 is a graph of the upward trajectory of the frequency of people searching for "employee experience" on Google from 2004 to 2023.

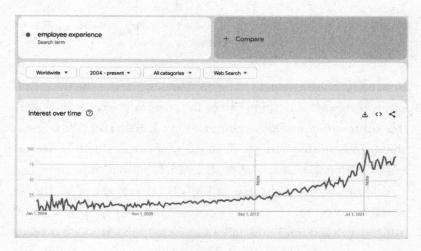

FIGURE 1-2

There is no denying that if you want to create a customer-focused company, you must start with your employees. Anyone can be a manager of people, but not everyone is a leader. When I talk about customer-focused leadership in this book, what I am also talking about is employee-focused leadership. You cannot have one without the other.

Since I started covering this area, customer experience has grown by leaps and bounds. Figure 1-3 shows the popularity of the search term "customer experience" on Google from 2004 to October 2023.

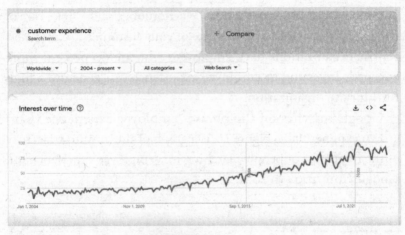

FIGURE 1-3

My first book was called *More Is More*, the "more" being enthusiasm and hard work on behalf of the customer. My second book, *The Customer of the Future*, came out in fall 2019 and talked about the digital transformation side of customer experience. The opening of the book said evolve or die, which is what most of us had to do just a few months later as COVID upended our businesses and lives.

Over the last ten years, talk of customer experience has made its way to the boardroom as more leaders become interested in serving their customers. One survey found that of companies with the CEO directly involved in customer experience, 83 percent increased customer satisfaction and 58 percent increased revenue associated with customer experience.[5]

While leaders can't single-handedly make a company customer centric, they set the tone and example for customer centricity. Sixty-four percent of companies with a customer-focused CEO are more profitable than their competitors.[6] I was recently asked at a leadership workshop for one of the largest telcos in the US if customer experience could be built from the bottom up. My answer was no. Leaders are the individuals that set the sails for the company, and all ships and passengers follow. If employees work long hours to create a customer-centric culture but they aren't appreciated or recognized by leadership, eventually they will get burned out and leave.

Leadership is the most important part of any business. People are often promoted to managers because they are good at their jobs. But not all managers are great leaders—and not all leaders understand how to run a customer-focused company. Today's modern leader must be excited and willing to talk to the customer themselves to get to the honest answer about how the brand is doing. They have to be the bosses that are out on the floor with everyone else, not locked away in an office somewhere. Think of the extremely approachable CEO Tricia Griffith of Progressive Insurance who has led the company through a huge amount of success (we will talk more about her in chapter 4). Here is someone that simply strolls up to the lunch tables at Progressive's Ohio headquarters, sits down, and has lunch every Friday with one lucky random group of employees. How many of your CEOs do that? Progressive's stock has skyrocketed since she became the leader.

Think back to the bosses you cherished (assuming you've been lucky enough to have a few good bosses)—did you feel they were right there alongside you? Best-case scenario is they didn't seem too good to do the work you were asked to do. They taught you how to do something, and, more importantly, you felt camaraderie with them. These bosses were flipping burgers alongside you, not leaving you alone in the kitchen.

Not all of my best bosses were nice. Some weren't even likable, but I learned from each one of them. I trusted most of them so when they gave me painful feedback I wasn't personally offended by it, and I used it to learn. These bosses came in all shapes and sizes, and were from all walks of life. But the one common denominator was they cared, and they cared about me and were willing to coach me. It made all the difference.

Customer experience isn't a fancy contact center flow chart. It's also not a customer loyalty framework. Customer experience is a decision you must make every single day. You have to wake up and decide to be a leader, which is not always easy. As you transform your work and become a customer-centric leader, you will find the fabric of your life transforms too.

People skills in leadership have never been more critical than they are now. The world is messy and needs strong leadership. It needs confidence, wisdom, humility, thoughtfulness, and integrity.

Leaders determine an organization's priorities. They are in charge of shaping the company culture, corporate values, how much money gets spent, and where that money goes.

When companies do well, all eyes are on the CEO and leadership team. And when companies do badly, all eyes are on the CEO and leadership team.

When Southwest Airlines left hundreds of thousands of customers stranded over the holidays in 2022 and their only communicated response simply blamed the weather, the world got angry. No one criticized the contact center agents or the pilots; they pointed the finger at CEO Robert Jordan. Pilots wrote long letters about being the canary in the coal mine, trying to warn management about the outdated technology they were limping along with. Scathing articles were written accusing the CEO of running the company like a CFO. When a company is losing money, it hires a new CEO. When a sports team keeps losing, it hires a new head coach. A great coach can turn around an average team, but even a team of high performers can't win if the coach isn't a good leader.

In the book *Extreme Ownership,* Jocko Willink and Leif Babin describe "hell week" training for Navy SEALs. As part of the training, the SEALs participate in a grueling boat race. In one incident, they described a boat that lagged behind, and the team was described as low performers. The Navy SEAL leaders decided to try an experiment and changed out the leaders. They put the high-performing coach with the low-performing team and the low-performing coach with the high-performing team. The low-performing team ended up outperforming the high-performing team. That's the power and impact of great leaders.

Leaders today need to be coaches, because employees need more engagement than they did in the past. One reason for this is with so many employees working remotely now, they've lost that excitement and spirit that comes from working together in person. Employees today are stressed, overwhelmed, and disengaged—and it's even worse for employees in customer-facing roles. Seventy-six percent of contact center agents report a negative impact on their quality of life due to stress.[7] Some of that stress can come from frustration with their job, but much of it comes from feeling unempowered and unsupported in their jobs. That's where leaders need to show up and provide the support, tools, and coaching employees need to feel comfortable at work and do their job well. The research is clear: engaged employees create better customer experiences. According to *Harvard Business Review,* companies that lead in employee experience develop more successful innovations and have Net Promoter Scores—which is how likely you are to recommend a company on a scale of 0 to 10—that are twice as high as their competitors who don't focus on employee experience.[8]

According to PwC, companies that invest in and deliver superior experiences to both customers and employees are able to charge a premium of as much as 16 percent for their products and services. That all starts with leaders who understand that people and relationships are their most crucial investments. Consider this staggering stat that Tom Goodmanson, the founder and former CEO of customer experience software provider Calabrio, shared with me in an interview: It costs $10,000 to change out a call center agent. If you have a contact center of a thousand and 30 percent turnover, it will cost you $3 million. You can save $100,000 for every 10 percent you reduce turnover. But still, companies continue to avoid investing in their contact center staff, even though this is often the customer's only experience interacting with the brand. Not investing in the contact center is a huge customer experience mistake.

CUSTOMER EXPERIENCE IS A DAILY DECISION

One of your hardest jobs is to inspire greatness in yourself. If you want to be a customer-centric leader, it starts with you! Being a dependable person starts with holding the commitments you make to yourself. You must hold yourself to a high standard every single day. You must work hard every day to find your *why*, dig deep to find empathy for your employees and customers, and be curious about your teams' experiences and your customers' experiences. Great leaders can paint the art of possibility for both employees and customers.

Customer experience doesn't happen in a vacuum. If individuals want to care more, they have to dig deep and find the strength and energy where they are lacking. Leaders can always work on themselves, no matter how successful they become. When I interviewed

Eduardo Briceño, author of the book *The Performance Paradox*, he talked about the idea of the growth mindset and how the commitment to working on yourself every day matters much more than natural talent. He brought up the example of Beyoncé, who records every show she performs and after the show, even though exhausted, goes to her hotel room, watches the playback, and takes notes on how the show can improve for the next night. She shares those notes with her team. Even Tom Brady is constantly learning new, healthy habits by talking to his teammates in the locker room to find out what they eat, drink, and what vitamins they take.

Many of these highly talented people the public assume are great because of a natural gift, but it's actually their tireless work ethic and growth mindset that make them successful. Individuals must work on themselves to develop the traits they need to become better leaders—customer-focused leaders. The work is never done—it's a wash, rinse, and spin approach to leadership. Somewhere in that cycle is talking to customers, something not all leaders commit to doing, and not often enough. According to *Harvard Business Review*, 72 percent of CEOs spend their time in meetings but only 3 percent with customers.[9] Leaders are not involved with customer experience strategy like they need to be, and that is why I've written this book. Customer experience is a discussion at the leadership level, and the top leaders at the company must take it seriously.

Customer experience is a discussion about believing in your work and making that work phenomenal, something you are proud of! It's a discussion about living with purpose. Customer experience is a philosophy on how to live. Customer experience is the art of caring about what you do all day. When you are engaged in your work, and you feel the work you do matters, you walk a little taller, have pep in your step, smile, and look forward to your work. You have purpose in your work, which creates meaning in your life. There are new laws for customer experience for a few reasons. One is that the pursuit of creating a good customer experience has a lot more awareness now than it did in the past. Sixty-three percent of CEOs want to rally organizations around customers as their top investment priority.[10] Gen Z is notably less satisfied with current customer experiences, with just 50 percent satisfaction compared to 71–72 percent for previous generations.[11] Increasingly, customer experience has moved up the chain, with a C-level officer responsible for it and a CEO interested in the outcome of these efforts. Gen Z expects more innovation and evolution of the companies they both work for and buy from—more so than any generation, and leaders today need to prepare for that.

And with economic uncertainty, the one thing you can count on is if you create more value for your customer, they will come back again and again. But if they feel you are not valuing the relationship, and not evolving or meeting them where they are, the customer will leave. I have personally just seen an explosion of the industry that helps build the customer experience—like software companies and companies that sell digital transformation—or even advertising focusing on it, where brands want customers to know they care about the experience and promise to deliver on it. Everyone wants to deliver an exceptional customer experience, but not everyone knows how to. I know that, because even you, dear reader, have probably had a terrible customer experience in the last week you could tell me about. But the rewards for customer-focused companies are many. One simple stat says it all: 89 percent of companies that lead with customer experience perform financially better than their competitors.[12]

With all that being said, I have spent years on this book researching, working with and advising clients, and understanding what the world's top customer-focused companies are doing. I have also had the unique opportunity to connect the conversation around leadership with the conversation around customer experience—something I have not seen enough attention paid to. I have distilled the many leadership principles of customer experience down to eight laws and mindsets. Each of the eight laws is explored in its own chapter. Let's jump in and take a quick look at each of the laws before we take a deep dive.

Law 1   Create a customer experience mindset. You can't ask your teams to do the work you're not willing to do. We'll examine how to model customer-focused leadership and look at examples of leaders who do this well.

Law 2   Exceed long-term profit expectations by balancing both short-term and long-term profits. Most companies aren't customer centric because they don't have a long-term vision. They can't think past what is happening this quarter. You'll learn how any leader today can and must think both short term and long term, and you will read examples of leaders that successfully do both.

Law 3   Lay out your customer experience strategy and stick to it. Everyone needs a vision—in this chapter I help you come up with a blueprint of what direction to drive and how to ensure you achieve alignment so the program sticks.

Law 4   Embark on your ninety-day get-started plan. We'll look at what you should be doing in your role, particularly in the first ninety days, and the tools and strategies for overcoming the resistance you might incur along your journey.

Law 5   Anticipate the future: be a customer experience futurist. You can't future-proof your company completely (anyone that tries to sell you this is lying), but you can learn to look at the tea leaves and predict the future in a more reliable way. Today, every leader must be a customer experience futurist to understand how to create the most modern, relevant, and enjoyable experience for your customer.

Law 6 Don't forget that employees are customers too. This is the biggest missing link for many companies. Employee and customer experience are linked. Delivering a solid, consistent customer experience isn't possible without engaged, empowered employees that have the tools they need to do their jobs. But how do you create an employee-focused culture that leads to better customer outcomes? In this chapter we'll look at beloved leaders who do this well.

Law 7 Evaluate success and measure what can be measured. There's a lot of disagreement when it comes to measurement. In this section, I'll help you understand what you should measure and what outcomes you can create based on different customer experience metrics. We'll look at a more modern approach to contact center metrics that *backs* into metrics by understanding the customer.

Law 8 Reaffirm the priority: keep customer experience front and center. Customer experience isn't a onetime decision. You need to keep it top of mind and likely bring others back to see the light of making decisions based on what is best for the customer.

When leaders relentlessly pursue an amazing customer experience based on the eight laws mentioned previously, even as the world and customers evolve, they spread that excitement and focus to the rest of their employees. And that's when the magic happens.

This book helps provide the road map to create a more customer-focused company. Each law includes a leadership scorecard where you can measure yourself along with many real-world examples of what customer-focused leadership looks like today from various types of companies. At the end of the book you can use my Customer-Centric Leadership scorecard (page 198) to gauge how you are doing and how far you have to go.

Just like Mel Fisher faced challenges in his hunt for the lost shipwreck, and Jeff Bezos faced criticism in Amazon's early days, so, too, will today's customer-focused leaders have struggles. But with an eye on what really matters—leading your employees and serving your customers—every day you can find that treasure chest and share the gold with everyone in your company.

Are you ready to dive into the adventure of a lifetime? It's time to become a customer-focused leader.

2

The Current State of Customer Experience

An in-home technician installed a new alarm system for an elderly couple. When the technician did the tour of the home, he noticed the basement did not have a carbon sensor or alarm installed. He mentioned his concern to the customers and emphasized the importance of a carbon alarm sensor, but they didn't seem very worried. They simply wanted him to get the traditional alarm system installed in the rest of the house and that's it. The basement they wanted untouched (but also unsecured).

But the ADT technician was a volunteer fireman and knew the dangers of not having a carbon sensor in all areas of the home. He told the customers he refused to leave until it was installed in the basement. When they protested that they didn't want to pay for it, the ADT technician made the decision to pay for it himself. Seven years went by, and nothing happened. But one day, there was a carbon leak in the basement of this couple's house on a night their grandchildren were sleeping over. The carbon sensor worked perfectly—the alarm went off, and fire trucks arrived on the scene. The grandparents were in tears. Had the ADT technician not installed the carbon sensor, this family would not be here today.

If customer experience could boil down to one word it would be *accountability*. This accountability comes from the mindset of the individual. When your company has the customer experience mindset, you have teams of people who all have the mindset of accountability—and when you have achieved that, you are unstoppable.

In the ADT story, you have an employee that treated the customer's home as if it were their own, or that of their grandparents, parents, or children. So the question is, where do you find employees like this, or more importantly, how do you develop this type of accountability in your employees? The answer is mindset.

Every individual mindset is affected by the culture of the company, and that culture is created by the leaders. If you want to learn about everything that's going well and not well inside a company, you can get a sense of that by looking at the customer experience. If the customer experience is incredible, it's likely the leaders of that company have adopted a customer experience mindset throughout the company. Customer experience is the thing that every company wishes they did well, but very few actually do. Customer experience goes beyond efficiency; it is the way you make your customers feel. It is the brand—which is a very intangible word—but when customers feel it, they know it! Let's look at some of the most beloved brands in the last ten years. What did they do well?

If you look at *Fortune's* list of the world's most beloved brands, which is based on a survey of more than fifty thousand executives, what you find is the most powerful combination of their commitment to continual innovation—finding ways to remain relevant and add value to the customer's life—and their amazing service, fulfilling the brand promise to the customer. They have not only worked hard to create incredible products, but they have gained trust with customers over the years by never compromising their customer relationships. Or if they do something bad, they apologize and fix it. Just look at Delta. Delta is number twelve on the list of *Fortune*'s most admired list, but in the fall of 2023 they really angered customers over changes to the loyalty program. They simply made it much harder to get status with the airline.

The CEO spoke out after an overwhelming amount of negative feedback from customers: "No question we probably went too far in doing that," CEO Ed Bastian told the Atlanta Rotary Club, according to the Associated Press. "I think we moved too fast, and we are looking at it now."[1]

It's not about not making mistakes; that is not reality. But it's how leadership addresses mistakes when they are made that makes all the difference. Customer service in particular has the biggest opportunity to build relationships with customers. Think of a time you've had a fight with a friend, and afterward the two of you actually got closer. Why did you get closer? Well, ideally you are able to talk through a disagreement, and afterward you both feel heard. We live in a society where people often don't feel heard, seen, or understood. If you can do that for someone then you are providing not just a transaction, but you've elevated the relationship and helped them feel better. It's amazing how at times friction can actually lead to something positive.

Anyone can set out to achieve a particular plan; however, the decisions you make when your plans don't work out like you intended make all the difference. How do I know plans will not go as intended all the time? I know this because there are human beings involved, not robots. And life and business can be messy, no matter how hard you try to create order and process. This book is not an equation for how to create or manage a customer experience program that's foolproof; the book discusses tactics for when things go wrong. Because that's life—things go wrong.

WHAT IS A CUSTOMER-CENTRIC LEADER?

A customer-centric leader places the needs, aspirations, and experiences of customers at the core of every decision, ensuring that organizational strategies not only drive business growth but also cultivate authentic relationships and lasting value for the people that they serve.

In this book, we will be diving into my eight laws of customer-focused leadership. I have flown to the far corners of the earth and interviewed thousands of executives about what it means to be a customer-centric leader. In the acronym CX LEADER, I take you through what it takes to develop customer-focused leadership (see figure 2-1). The next eight chapters each look at one of these eight laws. Let's get started by looking at an overview of the eight aspects I've identified in my research as the key components.

C.reate a customer experience mindset

eX.ceed long-term profit expectations by focusing on both short-term and long-term profits

L.ay out your your customer experience strategy and stick to it

E.mbark on your ninety-day get-started plan

A.nticipate the future: be a customer experience futurist

D.on't forget that employees are customers too

E.valuate success and measure what can be measured

R.eaffirm the priority: keep customer experience front and center

FIGURE 2-1

1. **Create a customer experience mindset (chapter 3).** When you are a customer-focused company, you've created a culture that creates the outcomes you want. Creating a customer experience mindset is the most important step you will take in your efforts to create the company that attracts and retains customers. Leaders have mindsets and those mindsets cascade down to employees, which greatly affect the experience that customers have. Mindset is the most important piece of the puzzle and the most overlooked. In chapter 4 we'll look at Tricia Griffith, CEO of Progressive Insurance, and why she is always recognized as being one of the most customer-focused leaders out there.

2. **Exceed long-term profit expectations by balancing both short- and long-term profits (chapter 4).** The hardest part of leadership is holding two opposing ideas in your mind at the same time. But that's the job, and there have been leaders like David Cote, the former CEO of Honeywell, who managed to create strategies that help the company win in the short term while also thinking of tomorrow. What is it that leaders like David do to achieve both short-term and long-term results by doubling down on customer experience? Chapter 4 will dive into what David did differently than other CEOs—David used a mindset to shift from short-term to long-term thinking, which improved the company's market cap from $20 billion to $120 billion.

3. **Lay out your customer experience strategy creation and stick to it (chapter 5).** You need a goal to figure out where you're going and how you will get there. In chapter 5 you will see two different ways to work on your customer experience strategy whether you already have one that needs work or you are starting from scratch. In chapter 3, we'll look at the world of Marvel and how they successfully achieved a complete customer experience transformation and the outcome of that.

4. **Embark on your ninety-day get-started plan (chapter 6).** In chapter 6 we look at the ninety-day plan of some of the world's most successful chief customer officers and also look at the ninety-day plan of CEOs that have turned big ships to become more customer centric. The first ninety days can be the most critical. How you start makes a world of difference, and those first three months can set you up for success. You need a strategy for your ninety-day get-started plan. It's possible you picked up this book because you started in a new role where you're tasked with building a customer strategy—this chapter will help you get started with a tangible strategy you can create on one piece of paper.

5. **Anticipate the future by being a customer experience futurist (chapter 7).** A futurist is someone that looks at possible scenarios of what can unfold and prepares business and society for those potential outcomes. As a leader you also have to be a futurist, particularly when you think about your customer strategy. How do you keep the company healthy now while also anticipating the future and where the company needs to be headed? Almost every industry will be forever changed by incredible advances in technology and generative AI. This chapter gives you some practical ideas and ways of thinking to get started to ensure you are disrupting yourself before another business disrupts you. In this chapter we'll also go through a futurist exercise together of horizon scanning that you can do at your own company.

6. **Don't forget that employees are customers too (chapter 8).** The world is facing a disengagement crisis right now. The first place to start on your journey to becoming a customer-focused company is inside your own company—with your employees. Your employees are the keys to an improved customer experience, but many leaders forget that. Employee engagement is very low today globally. You can't expect to build any kind of compelling customer experience when your employees have checked out.

Engaging employees is the biggest missed opportunity staring you right in the face. Later in this book you'll learn employee engagement strategies from the world's top coaches and leaders.

7. **Evaluate success and measure what can be measured (chapter 9).** Measuring the wrong metrics is the top challenge that I see facing leaders globally. Many companies still view the contact center as a cost center. With modern technology you have the ability to measure almost everything in your business, but if it were so easy wouldn't customer experiences be better across the board? Many customer experience leaders are still managing their programs with an outdated view on metrics that doesn't account for the modern customer. Having the right metrics in place can make or break your customer strategy. For too long this topic has been full of misinformation that keeps customer programs small. This chapter on measurement is closely linked with the chapter on profits. The more you can show the success you're having with customer programs, the more likely you will get more money for your customer programs. Measuring customer experience is one of the most challenging issues out there. Let's bring some sanity back to customer experience measurement, in particular in the contact center.

8. **Reaffirm the priority: keep CX front and center (chapter 10).** Many well-intended companies launch customer experience programs only to let them lose momentum and gather dust as other initiatives take precedent. To keep customer experience as a central theme, your company has to continue to create the customer experience mindset in its culture. In this chapter you will learn about companies that have been successful at continuing to maintain a customer focus even as they grow and scale.

As the world and markets evolve, every business has become a commodity. Today, brands compete on experience more than price or product. And building a great experience and the customer experience mindset starts by understanding the modern customer. But it's more than that—it's also modeling great leadership for employees and then setting employees up for success so they can carry out the best service. Your experience is your product, and that has very big implications for every modern business today that wants to remain relevant.

NEW SURVEY CONDUCTED WITH MORE THAN ONE THOUSAND CUSTOMER EXPERIENCE LEADERS

To better understand the state of customer-focused leadership, in the summer of 2023, I partnered with global leadership firm DDI to survey nearly a thousand leaders from more than five hundred organizations and twenty-four major industry sectors around the globe. This was done as a part of DDI's Global Leadership Forecast Series, which is the longest-running global study of current and future leadership best practices. What we found was that there is still much work to do in the next few years, but the awareness of what needs to happen in customer experience is starting to gain traction.

Here are six key findings from the DDI survey:

1. **Leaders Are Not Spending Enough Time Mentoring Employees.** Although 76 percent of respondents say that senior leadership communicates that customer experience is a priority, *only* 42 percent say that their senior or executive leaders regularly spend time with customer-facing employees.

   What it means: Executives still say that customer experience is a priority, but they are not making the commitment that is necessary by actually talking to customers. They are not flipping burgers or spending time working in the contact center to talk to customers. Making customer experience a priority requires many internal business shifts, including resources allocated, organizational structure, engineering processes, and much more. Saying you want to be customer centric but not reducing back-end complexity or operational efficiencies, or making sure your employees have what they need to do their job, is not going to help.

2. Leaders Are Not Investing in Their People. Only 35 percent say that employees are viewed as customers.

What it means: While companies want to level up the experience of customers, most are not willing to make the investment in their people. Additionally, while many blame the turnover in customer-facing employees on COVID and quiet quitting, research after COVID from *Harvard Business Review* shows that it's actually wage stagnation as the reason most employees leave. A lack of engagement of employees will bring the demise of the business.[2]

3. Leaders Are Resource Poor. Only 68 percent of leaders feel well equipped to support their customers.

What it means: Budgets have been cut across the board, putting pressure on leaders to do more with less. This is a glaring gap in customer experience: the groups that have been put in charge of anything with the word *customer* in front of it do not have the resources they need to help the customer. So the question each leader must ask themselves is, why not? Once you start doing root-cause analysis on why your staff are underresourced to serve your customers, you will start to understand why your company isn't currently more customer centric. The answer will guide you to chapter 4 where we talk about short- versus long-term profits and why you need to invest in both.

4. **Leaders Are Not Able to Effectively Track the ROI of Customer Experience.** Fewer than half (40 percent) of leaders said that their company tracks the ROI of customer experience.

What it means: Most companies have not figured out how to track the ROI of creating better experiences for customers. If businesses want the customer experience to be incredible, they have to pay attention to it. They say energy flows where attention goes. Money also flows where attention goes, and if you do not give your ROI equation any attention, there will be no money flowing. In the book you will see ROI examples of proving you are either saving your company money or making your company money.

5. **There Is Not Alignment Across the Organization About Customer Experience Initiatives.** Forty-six percent of leaders said their customer experience initiatives have frequently been met with resistance.

What it means: The research says leaders are met with resistance almost half the time they try to make customer experience a bigger priority in their organization. If your colleagues are resisting your programs, it means they do not understand or see the value in supporting them. They do not know the WIIFM factor (what's in it for me?). You have to think like a salesperson and learn how to sell your ideas. You have to think like a politician, for better or worse. You can think of John Nash (remember the film *A Beautiful Mind*?) and understand how to convey that you are doing what is best for "me, you, and the group." Game theory is a theoretical framework for conceiving social situations among competing players. In some respects, game theory is the science of strategy, or at least the optimal decision-making of independent and competing actors in a strategic setting. This can be applied to customer experience strategy as well, or getting anything accomplished in an organization with leaders that have different priorities. You have to know how to get these individuals to care—and that's an art and a science.

6. When CX Leaders Are Frustrated with Lack of Support, They Quit. Eighty-seven percent of leaders who meet this kind of resistance have experienced decreased engagement or less likelihood to stay in the company.

What it means: There is a toll on leaders when they are not empowered or supported to create customer-centric companies. Simply put, poor customer experience is bad for employee morale. If day in and day out your employees' ideas are shot down, you can expect that over time employees are going to mentally check out. High employee engagement is good for customer experience, and good customer experience is good for employee engagement. Employees want to care about their work, and they want to win, but you have to give them the chance to try.

According to DDI in 2020, nearly a third of leaders felt *very* prepared to act on changing customer needs, but that number has since dropped to a mere 21 percent of leaders. Based on data gathered in DDI's Global Leadership Forecast study with fourteen thousand respondents, there's been a drop-off of 27 percent in the number of leaders feeling very prepared to act on changing customer needs since before COVID. This also reflects what Forrester analyst Pete Jacques told me when I interviewed him. Companies sprinted so fast to meet the customer where they were during COVID—investing millions of dollars on digital transformations and digital service—companies are drained. They want to spend money on other programs now and not on customer service.

CUSTOMER EXPERIENCE LAGGARDS WILL LAG, WHILE LEADERS GET STRONGER

Companies with highly rated customer experiences saw their stock performance increase 45 percent between 2019 and 2022, while companies with low customer experience ratings saw their stock returns decline 21 percent in the same time period.[3]

During uncertain times companies that never saw the value in customer experience are eager to cut customer programs. Think of companies like Frontier Airlines, which completely ditched their call center.[4] Forrester predicts that one in five customer experience programs will disappear, while one in ten will be stronger than ever.[5] That means the handful of companies that see the value in customer experience know this is their time to put the pedal to the metal and differentiate. When everyone goes left, they go right! Frontier is in contrast to a brand like Trader Joe's that does not use any self-checkout and whose people are Trader Joe's prime differentiators. We'll talk more in the book about the founder of Trader Joe's, Joe Coulombe, and how he instilled a customer and employee focus early on that is still alive and well today.

WHO IS THE MODERN CUSTOMER?

Customer demands and preferences are constantly changing, but perhaps never more than during and after the pandemic. Customers do not want to go back to the way things were, but companies are not rising to the occasion. In a postpandemic world, according to a recent HubSpot report, 90 percent of customer experience leaders say customer expectations have increased to an all-time high.[6] If you're working off old information or outdated assumptions, you're missing out on what today's customers want and demand in an experience.

The modern customer is:

- **Experience driven.** We are now in the experience economy, and modern customers often prioritize experiences over products. They seek memorable and meaningful interactions with brands, whether it's through unique in-store experiences or engaging online content. A recent Eventbrite survey discovered that roughly 78 percent of Millennials prefer experiences over products.[7]

- **Informed.** Customers have never had so much information at their fingertips. A staggering 81 percent of customers do research online before going to a store, and 56 percent of in-store shoppers use their phones to shop or research items while in the store. Modern customers use social media and rely on peer reviews and social proof when making buying decisions.[8]

- **Diverse needs and craves personalization.** Customers expect companies to do a better job of being inclusive of people from all walks of life and backgrounds. Additionally there is much more awareness now of how handicap accessible experiences are. Brands are held to a higher standard for how they create customer journeys.

- **Seeking convenience.** Customers are getting a variety of experiences, and increasingly they prefer companies that provide convenience and time-saving measures. Services like same-day delivery, one-click purchases, and subscription models have gained popularity.

- **Concerned about sustainability.** Customers today, in particular Gen Z, are extremely concerned about environmental challenges like climate change. The media is creating an extreme amount of stress in people, in particular young people. Customers today want brands to not "greenwash" issues but help provide actually useful global solutions.

- **Not married to any particular brand.** The modern customer is much less loyal than they used to be. With so many options, customers can easily change brands and companies after a single bad experience—and 63 percent will leave after one bad experience.[9]

- **Connected.** Buying decisions don't happen in a vacuum. Many customers today are digital natives, having grown up with technology. Customers are connected to their peers, other brands, and the news. They listen to other people's opinions and want to share their own ideas. To connect with a customer, you also have to connect with their network and be relevant in their hyperconnected world. That means authenticity and digital connections have never been more important.

- **Security and privacy conscious.** Today modern customers are vigilant about their personal information, and they have reason to be—there is an increasing amount of data breaches. In 2022, according to Statista, there were eighteen hundred data compromises affecting 450 million people.[10] Customers expect companies to prioritize data security and respect their privacy. Consider the rise in data breaches after 2020 in figure 2-2.

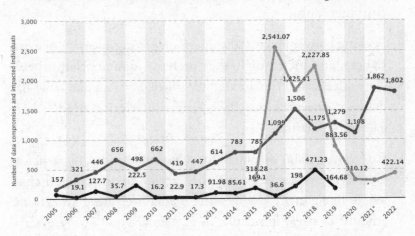

FIGURE 2-2

HOW IS TECHNOLOGY DISRUPTING CUSTOMER EXPERIENCE?

At the core of every change to customer experience over the last decade has been technology. And while adjusting to new digital tools brings challenges and a learning curve, it also allows brands to connect with their customers in a more personalized and scalable way. Instead of spending time to create individual messages for each customer—or giving every customer the same canned experience—tools like AI and machine learning help brands reach more customers in the way that resonates most with them, all while having a better and more accurate view of data.

There's incredible potential for things like AI, VR, and AR to transform how people shop and interact with brands. And with technology advancing and more brands expanding their AI and AR use, this is just the beginning of empowering, tech-enabled experiences.

But there are also significant challenges and roadblocks. Chat-GPT has been a major disruption to customer experience, for both good and bad. ChatGPT understands natural language and improves with every use, which is why brands like Duolingo, Expedia, my client Globe (Filipino telecom and tech company), and Coca-Cola have integrated it into their customer experience and marketing strategies. But it isn't a perfect solution: ChatGPT doesn't have special training into every brand and industry and can sometimes provide inaccurate and unreliable information.

A customer-centric mindset can and should spread through the entire company. It's the foundation of how work is done every day.

HOW WOULD THESE DEPARTMENTS LOOK DIFFERENT WITH A CUSTOMER MINDSET?

Human resources. Creating a company-wide customer obsession starts with hiring the right people, and a customer-centric HR department understands its essential role. A customer-centric HR department considers soft skills when hiring people who genuinely like people. It prioritizes hiring people who have the servant leadership mentality in their DNA. The HR team has a constant eye on changing customer tastes and societal needs and matches that with the skills and mindsets it finds in new hires. The new hire onboarding looks different as HR considers employees' initial experience and how to showcase the customer-focused way of doing business from day one.

Leadership development. Customer-centric companies don't leave leadership development up to chance. They systemize leadership development to build a pipeline of customer-centric leaders at every level. These programs train leaders to think with an outside-in perspective and teach them to balance the stress of the short term with the vision of long-term goals. These companies develop leaders internally and hire great leaders externally who are innately curious about problem-solving and are willing to flip burgers with their teams.

Sales. A customer-focused sales team spends time understanding customers' needs. They don't simply try to sell as much volume as possible but consider the individual needs of the client. A customer-centric sales team uses technology to determine the customers' future needs and stay one step ahead. One example is USAA, which leverages AI to find patterns that indicate major life events in its customers' lives, such as a deployment or sending a child to college. As customers approach these milestones, USAA meets them with fully mapped-out service offerings catered to their needs. When a customer buys a home, USAA is ready with loan information, home insurance, and guidance about the entire process. As customers near retirement, USAA representatives share a library of information, as well as recommend insurance and banking changes for a new stage of life.

Finance. Customer experience and finance are often pitted against each other as CX teams try to show the impact of their initiatives on the bottom line. But that's not the case with the customer experience mindset. The most successful customer-focused executives partner with finance to get the support they need to articulate the business case and ROI of investing in customer programs. When JPMorgan CEO Jamie Dimon invested $12 billion on a digital transformation in 2022, it's safe to assume his CFO was involved in identifying that budget. When I interviewed Chase's chief design officer, Kaaren Hanson, in the winter of 2023, she shared that a lot of this money went to paying the talent that builds technology experiences for customers.

Operations. This is the surprisingly important piece of customer experience that can make or break a company's customer initiative. Operations is where the rubber meets the road and strategy becomes reality. Even just considering the idea of a digital transformation is possible only with a leader who takes into account all of the business's needs and ensures customers receive products and services in a fast, modern, seamless, and frictionless manner. A customer-focused operations department considers the impact its processes and systems will have on customers and employees and works to cut red tape and make things as streamlined as possible for both sides.

Marketing. Marketing is often the department that drives and oversees customer experience. But in a customer-centric organization, marketing works closely with other departments, especially the contact center. Marketing is the department that also owns the relationship with the customer, along with customer service. For example, Darren MacDonald, chief customer officer of Petco, runs marketing; the chief marketing officer reports to him.

Customer service. *Customer experience is the best marketing money can't buy.* But one thing the company can do is invest in the place that has the power to shape the customer experience in a very tangible way. The contact center is how most customers interact with the brand. It plays a huge role in how customers view your company and their overall experience. Companies with a customer experience mindset make customer service and the contact center a priority and think of it as an opportunity center, not a cost center. One of the best examples of a well-run contact center is Capital One, which allows their contact center agents the budget and freedom to block and tackle for the customer. While they track all traditional metrics, Capital One doesn't tightly control the contact center by measuring how long it takes for agents to go to the bathroom (many companies actually do this). As a result, the contact center stories are the stuff of legends and are often featured in media and TV—that's huge for employee morale and for building Capital One's customer-focused reputation.

IN THE NEXT chapter we explore the first law of the customer-focused leader—how to embody the customer experience mindset. It's not mastered by many companies. If it were, every company would have absolutely perfect customer experiences and service, and I wouldn't need to speak at conferences or write this book. But there is still much work to be done, so roll your sleeves up. It's time to get fixing. Let's dive into Law 1, Create a Customer Experience Mindset.

3

Law 1: Create a Customer Experience Mindset

*I don't open restaurants;
I tell stories, and no two are alike.*
—CHEF JOSÉ ANDRÉS

For years many people have tried to define customer experience—and describe it. But there has simply been so much confusion about something that is actually very simple. Customer experience is not a division at your company. One group cannot own it. Customer experience is not a discipline. You cannot learn it in school. Customer experience is just a decision; but it's a decision you have to make every day.

There has never been a more important time to make the customer experience mindset decision. Based on post-COVID trends from DDI—the research agency I partnered with for my book—leaders reported lack of confidence in being able to keep up with and act on changing customer needs. Coupled with growing economic uncertainty and the tremendous amount of change that's happened (including technology and digital transformation), leaders do not feel prepared to deal with what's in front of them.

According to the broader DDI leadership survey with fourteen thousand practitioners, there's been a 17 percent decline in confidence in the leaders above them. This lack of confidence in themselves combined with a lack of confidence in the people driving is a recipe for disaster. Executives do not feel equipped to deal with modern customer challenges, and they don't trust their bosses either.[1]

According to this same survey, fewer than one in three employees (32 percent) said they trust senior leaders within their organization. Let's repeat this—most employees don't trust their senior leadership to do what's right for them as employees. They don't trust their bosses. And, according to DDI researchers, that also means they may not do what's right for their customers.

Think about that for a minute: after COVID, businesspeople felt less confident in their ability to solve problems and even less confident in their bosses and higher-ups' ability to solve problems for employees and customers. If leaders are not actively solving gaps in customer experience, why would the employees that report to them show the extreme ownership necessary?

But there are outliers that are walking to the beat of their own drums. These companies are using game theory, doing what is best for the company, employees, and customers. They are investing in long-term programs, processes, and operational efficiencies that in the short term aren't that efficient. They are doing this because they know that investing in customer experience will have payoffs. These are the world's most beloved brands.

According to Deloitte, client-focused companies are 60 percent more profitable than companies not focused on the customer.[2] What I've found is that all of these companies have customer-centric leaders. These leaders chose to be customer centric over being product centric. They looked outward rather than inward.

Customer experience is the great leveling field of our time. Any small group can build an experience that people hate, reconstruct it with a better experience for the customer, and be the new big fish. No company—no matter how big or old it is—is safe from being disrupted.

Business is a meritocracy. You can achieve both short-term profits as well as long-term goals. The minute it stops innovating for customers, any company can disappear. And any leader can write themselves out of the story. Today's changing world demands engaged leaders that are paying attention, that care greatly about those on the receiving end of an experience.

And it turns out mindset is important. Mindset affects our worldview, how we think, how we talk, how we treat our teams, and the culture (or you can call it vibe) we create in our companies.

Being a customer-centric leader means you feel extreme ownership over your work. You make the decision every day to be better than average—you choose to balance short-term goals with long-term strategies. The customer-centric leader works arduously to understand their customers and create experiences based on actual feedback of what customers would like to see. Seventy-two percent of business executives say, "We understand what it feels like to be one of our customers." But only 35 percent of consumers say that companies "understand me well."[3]

STORYTELLING WITH STYLE—MARVEL ENTERTAINMENT STUDIOS

It might surprise you to learn that in the late 1990s and early 2000s Marvel Entertainment Studios was running out of money and on the brink of bankruptcy.* The company was desperate and even sold the film rights to some of its most popular characters, including Spider-Man and the X-Men. Backed into a corner,

---

* In 2024, Marvel has had some challenges as well, but they've already overcome trials and tribulations in the past. I'm sure that if they apply their customer experience savvy, they can get back to where they once were.

Marvel decided it needed an Iron Man injection of energy and decided to relaunch the company with a customer experience mindset.

Here were the big steps they took:

1. **Strategically restructured their organization:** Marvel underwent a significant corporate restructuring, streamlining operations and cutting costs. This helped them reduce debt.

2. **Focused and doubled down on their best products:** Instead of offering watered-down versions of many characters, Marvel focused on producing high-quality comic books featuring their iconic superheroes. They reinvigorated interest in their best-loved characters with new story arcs and narratives.

3. **Overmanaged the things they care about.** Marvel brought its movie productions in-house: instead of licensing its characters to other studios, Marvel decided to produce its own movies. They formed Marvel Studios as a subsidiary to oversee the development and production of their films.

4. **Disrupted themselves by reimagining the world of their characters with style, fun, freshness, and creativity.** Marvel used creativity to do something others were not doing. Traditionally each character lived in their own narrative, but Marvel combined narratives and created a shared cinematic universe for its characters, where individual films would be interconnected, leading to crossover events and team-up movies. This cohesive storytelling approach created new buzz and viral excitement for fans that had never seen anything like this.

5. **Refocused on experiential marketing.** Strategic film releases: Marvel began tapping into experiential marketing by releasing

films strategically, building up anticipation and excitement for their interconnected movies. They carefully planned character introductions and storylines to keep fans engaged and invested in the larger narrative.

6. **Took risks and made thoughtful bets.** Marvel took creative risks by hiring relatively unknown directors and actors for some of their early films. This allowed them to attract top talent at a lower cost and bring fresh perspective to their superhero films.

The result of this commitment to customer experience mindset was a remarkable turnaround for Marvel Entertainment: box office success. The release of *Iron Man* in 2008 marked the beginning of Marvel's transformative success that set up a string of successful superhero films. Marvel was acquired one year later by Disney for $4 billion.

The new format with interconnected storytelling captured the imagination of audiences worldwide, leading to a massive fan following and significant box office revenue. The success allowed Marvel to diversify its offerings, including TV shows, animated series, merchandise, and video games. Marvel's turnaround story demonstrates how a commitment to innovation powered by the customer experience mindset leads to creativity, risk-taking, and immense success and growth for a company. The Marvel Cinematic Universe has become a cultural phenomenon and has redefined the landscape of superhero movies and the entertainment industry as a whole.

So how does every company take a page out of Marvel's book, to turn a ship so effortlessly when they've already established a culture? They can follow the strategy that Marvel embraced (see figure 3-1).

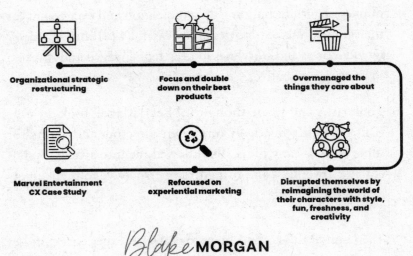

Organizational strategic restructuring

Focus and double down on their best products

Overmanaged the things they care about

Marvel Entertainment CX Case Study

Refocused on experiential marketing

Disrupted themselves by reimagining the world of their characters with style, fun, freshness, and creativity

Blake MORGAN

FIGURE 3-1

THE ENERGY FOR INFLUENCING CHANGE

I didn't make up this phrase, "the energy for influencing change." It was given to me by Donna Morris, the chief people officer for Walmart. When I worked with her, she was the CHRO and CXO at Adobe. Donna is known for many things, but at the time she was most known for throwing out the annual employee review. In 2012, during a business trip to India, Donna vented her frustrations over traditional performance management. Jet lag emboldened her, and in an interview she told a reporter that the company planned to abolish annual reviews and stack rankings in favor of more frequent, forward-facing feedback. But she hadn't yet discussed it with her HR staff or with Adobe's CEO. With characteristic energy and persuasiveness, Donna hustled to bring the company around.[4] She felt the reviews were no longer relevant and were just a "cumbersome process" they were doing because they always did it. Her discussions around this topic were unprecedented at the company and in the industry. Donna is an example of how, if you have the energy for influencing change, you will never be without a leadership opportunity. Sometimes long-standing rules and practices—especially in the contact center—must be thrown out. In order to be bold you must have the energy for influencing change. If you don't have the energy, you better start working on developing your energy levels and your appetite for change.

The following eight steps stand out as critical ways to create the customer experience mindset for yourself. These eight steps (see also figure 3-2) can give you a big boost with your own leadership—to truly become a customer-centric leader and embody the customer-focused mindset.

8 Mindsets of the Customer Experience Leader

1 Flip burgers and take out trash next to employees

2 Give no excuses

3 Commit to excellence

4 See feedback as a chance for growth

5 Don't take yourself too seriously

6 Believe employees are the path

7 Know that everything you do matters

8 Have a life outside of work

Blake **MORGAN**

FIGURE 3-2

1. Flip burgers next to employees.

The customer experience mindset means you are an in-the-trenches kind of leader. You are a coach that is doing drills next to your team members. You are not above the work you ask others to do. They see you as someone that's approachable, that understands the importance of camaraderie and approachability.

2. Give no excuses.

The customer experience mindset is when a leader decides to be accountable. While the problem might not be your fault—and you cannot control the behavior of others—you are accountable for always doing your best in that moment. If you always do your best, and you leave nothing on the mat, then you should always be able to sleep at night. Giving no excuses means this willingness to take ownership and to not pass the buck or blame others. If you want accountability and ownership from your team, then you better show that yourself. It also means not complaining or bad-mouthing anyone and sticking to your word. It means you have a strong say-do ratio, because you always do what you say you're going to do. Even if you are blamed for something that is not your fault, people always can tell what kind of person you are. If you have a reputation for fair decision-making and honest behavior, then you will never have a problem.

3. Commit to excellence.

While perfection is not possible in modern life, aspiring for zero defects or unforced errors is. A commitment to excellence is simply the act of always doing your best. People settle for whatever standards are set around them. I was recently at a fine dining restaurant in Los Angeles. The decor was beautiful, and clearly a lot of effort had been put into the design of the restaurant. And the food was expensive—one steak cost seventy dollars. But as I sat, I turned to my left and saw a thick layer of dust on a shelf at my eye level. I couldn't let that go. It put a bad taste in my mouth for the entire meal. I thought, how can they charge so much for their food when they don't keep the restaurant tidy? It only takes one sloppy piece of an experience to ruin it.

Consider the commitment to perfectionism of Walt Disney: he challenged his Imagineers (designers) when they were creating the first animatronics for the Enchanted Tiki Room. As noted in Will Guidara's book *Unreasonable Hospitality: The Remarkable Power of Giving People More Than They Expect*, the Imagineers were convinced they had produced the most lifelike, detailed animatronic bird possible, but Walt Disney wasn't happy with them. Real birds' chests expand and contract, he pointed out; real birds breathe. This bird wasn't breathing. The Imagineers were frustrated, and they reminded him there would be hundreds of distracting elements in the Tiki Room, including waterfalls, lights, smoke, totem poles, and singing flowers—nobody was going to notice a single bird, whether it was breathing or not. To which Disney responded, "People can feel perfection." Maybe people don't notice every single individual detail, but in aggregate, they're powerful. These small touches cumulatively create the customer experience.[5]

4. See feedback as a chance for growth.

There are two mindsets when it comes to feedback. The CTB mindset, and the CTI mindset. CTB means "check the box" mindset. CTI means "chance to improve" mindset. Today you have the opportunity to use a mix of quantitative and qualitative data, looking at actual feedback but also using technology to plow through the language of how customers speak. Every week as a leader you need to be talking to customers or organizing a customer advisory board. You should have customers that you talk to all the time to learn what's actually happening on the ground. Don't depend on others to feed you distant survey feedback—ensure that you are looking at actual feedback and data all the time. If the data is wrong or not dependable, you should say something. The feedback should not be seen as a pain—because the company must change—but as a chance to improve. Amazon asks every employee one question every day, and they plow through that feedback with machine learning and AI to ensure employees don't have roadblocks in front of them.

5. Don't take yourself too seriously.

The customer experience mindset doesn't take itself too seriously. That means that when a leader messes up, they can admit it. Ego does not get in the way. Also, the customer-focused leader is a coach that knows how to lighten the mood in a room. If you are moving fast and taking risks—part of the customer experience mindset—then you must be prepared that things will go wrong. At times you will lose. And that's an important piece of customer-focused leadership. A sense of humor can help relax everyone, even you. When you are relaxed and humble enough to admit when you goof, or laugh at yourself, it creates a better culture all around you.

Mentally coaching yourself through ups and downs is a big part of taking risks and winning. Throughout the book you will see stories of leaders that exhibit this trait in the "storytelling with style" section. Many of the world's most compelling business leaders are quirky, humble, but strong as hell. They do hard things. In the book you will read about modern leaders who are living the customer experience mindset and doing it with their own style. In the near future every customer experience will be improved by technology—experiences will get faster, more accurate, intuitive, and seamless. An example is Fifth Third Bank, where Vice Chairmen Tim Welsh and John Elmore started wearing red shoes as a symbol of a newfound spirit to be bold and different. This was a reminder of the bank's need to transform, and eventually hundreds of employees started wearing red shoes. Eventually every company will have these technologies, so you will not just be competing on speed, efficiency, and accuracy. You will need to compete on something more. You will need to determine what that "something more" is at your company.

Leaders with the customer experience mindset embrace being human. Aiming for perfection is one thing, but an obsession with perfectionism kills innovation. If leaders can lighten up and incorporate some fun and whimsy into the way they lead, they will create a more open culture, a culture where people feel more comfortable being bold, taking risks, and speaking up when something could go very wrong.

My most memorable bosses weren't robots. They colored outside the lines, showed up as their full selves at work, and even embraced vulnerability at times. They used storytelling and whatever they had to do to lead their teams and convey their messages. These leaders were giants in my mind and in my memory, not because they said the right thing every time but because they were dynamic human beings, and most of all they cared enough to create a culture that was real and welcoming.

6. Believe employees are the path.

Restaurateur Danny Meyer was radical in how he prioritized the people who worked at his restaurants over everything else, including the guests and the investors. This didn't mean the customer suffered; in fact, the opposite. Danny's big idea was to hire great people, treat them well, and invest deeply into their personal and professional growth knowing they would take great care of the customers—which is exactly what they did. A customer-focused mindset is laser focused on what is happening with employees. The employee is the path to the customer.

7. Know that everything you do matters.

Creating a mindset for excellence starts with you. You can't just be an incredible leader and leave your family life a mess, not take care of yourself physically or mentally, and avoid taking care of your personal life. Being a customer-centric leader means that you understand getting out of bed in the morning is a privilege that others were not given. You show up every day for everyone in your life with honor, respect, grace, and gratitude. You shine your shoes, brush your teeth, put on your big girl pants, and do the hard things that you don't always feel like doing (with enthusiasm).

8. Have a life outside of work.

When you're a leader, no one is going to take care of you. That is why *you* must take care of *you* so you have energy to give to others. If you don't inspire yourself daily and get yourself into a good mood that is grateful and happy, you have nothing to give others. The customer-centric leader is actually committed to themselves before anyone else. They understand they must spend their free time mentally and physically molding themselves into a leader. Sometimes that means getting a coach, friend, or therapist to help get you out of your head. Having support at home will make you less reliant on others at work.

You should be the same person to the colleagues above you, lateral to you, and below you. You should not gossip or fraternize with your colleagues in a way that makes you look bad. There is no excuse for you not being the person you are asking others to be. You must embody the values that you uphold. You must commit to keeping your mind and heart clear so you can lead others. You must have boundaries; you must make time for the things that make you feel focused and content—whether that's meditation, eating healthy, running outdoors, doing Zumba, blaring music, playing Frisbee with your dog at the beach, or playing pickleball. How about walking your dog, volunteering at a soup kitchen or animal shelter, spending time at your church or temple, or being with your family? Some people relax by singing in the shower or listening to music and dancing in their living room or watching stand-up comedy on YouTube.

You need an outlet for yourself outside of work that gives you energy for work. You cannot be the same person in every area of your life. It's your responsibility to find a place that fills your cup, that gives you energy, so you don't explode from stress or pressure. The customer-centric leader is an unwaveringly positive person: even though they have moments of stress and struggle, they prevail. This person has faith in their and others' ability to create good in this world. But they also take care of themselves first, knowing if they are in good condition they have more to offer the group.

Leaders must be willing to get off the hamster wheel long enough to take a look at what's working and what's not working. In the next chapter we'll look at leaders who do this, leaders in the C-suite and leaders of contact center operations. The truth is anyone can become customer centric, as long as they have the drive, the focus, and the willingness to do hard things. Being customer-focused means balancing short-term goals with long-term strategies.

Life should look like the infinity loop / number eight on the cover of this book. Taking time for yourself means you feel better, which means you have more positive energy for those around you, and your outcomes become better, which makes you feel better and want to continue to invest in yourself. The great job you do at work makes you feel good, and feeling good helps you do better at work.

When you care about your work, you bring your passion to your work—and your employees, colleagues, and customers benefit. But so do you!

IN THE BOOK *Setting the Table,* author and chairman of Shake Shack and Union Square Hospitality Group Danny Meyer—who we mentioned earlier—wrote about a couple celebrating their anniversary at one of his restaurants. Midway through their meal they were horrified to realize they left a bottle of champagne in their freezer. They called the sommelier over to ask if the bottle of champagne would explode before they got home. The sommelier shocked the couple by taking their keys and rescuing the bottle at their home. The couple could relax and finish their celebratory meal without worry. When they got home, they found the champagne safely tucked into their fridge, along with a tin of caviar, a box of chocolates, and an anniversary card from the restaurant. It's moments like this that ranked Eleven Madison Park first on the prestigious World's Best Restaurant list in 2017. Danny Meyer and Will Guidara worked together—Danny hired Will to open and run the restaurant. Will also wrote a book about it called *Unreasonable Hospitality: The Remarkable Power of Giving People More Than They Expect.*

Sometimes customers want something not on the menu (in the words of Eleven Madison Park restaurateur and author Will Guidara), and if you are able to accommodate them with a smile, it's likely you've created an advocate. Will, the general manager of Eleven Madison Park, used "surprise and delight" as a way to help his establishment become the World's Number One best restaurant. Guidara told me in an interview in the winter of 2023, "The only time I sat down with the team to talk about the budget for surprise and delight was when we weren't spending enough." Every day the team was asked to make one customer's day at the restaurant—and it paid off—but ROI was never the goal. Customers are shown to spend up to 140 percent more after a positive experience than customers who report negative interactions. Additionally, customers tell an average of nine people about a positive experience with a brand, but they tell sixteen people about a negative experience.[6]

Additionally, can you say the following statements are true for you?[7] If you can't , then you know where to start on your mindset work.

- Our people are the number one focus at our company.

- I am currently thinking and planning for where my company will be in five to ten years.

- I'm committed to the continuous evolution of how we hire, train, manage, and everything related to how we deliver products and services.

- We have developed educational programs for teams that include digital courses, live workshops, and ongoing nudges to support the development of customer programs.

- Managers regularly receive tips on how to support, accelerate, and celebrate customer centricity within the organization—for example, by integrating design thinking into the early stages of the strategic planning process.

- We've made a significant investment in recruiting and nurturing agile teams with deep expertise in experience design, developing cutting-edge omnichannel platforms and technology, and reimagining the experiences, products, and services that best deliver on the brand promise.

- I regularly show an interest and participate in customer-facing activities—and I'm not above flipping burgers next to staff.

Many of you reading this book watch movies about superheroes. You see the millions of articles written about professional athletes, about Nobel Prize winners, about famous actors that are worshipped. But today's modern superhero is a humble leader that takes care of the people in their care. They understand how critical it is that people with leadership qualities hone those skills and give back to the people around them. We are facing uncertain times, and only more crazy stuff happens out of left field. We need better leadership today.

Even though you can't immediately see, hear, or feel the energy in the room when you show brave, bold, courageous, and kind leadership, the energy is there, and that energy dictates the future. Every day, you are making a decision—a decision to have the customer experience mindset or not.

IN THIS CHAPTER we looked at the eight qualities for the customer experience mindset. We looked at examples of what customer experience mindset looks like out in the world. Now you're ready to start thinking about building the business case. It's time to learn how to hold two opposing ideas in your mind at one time: short-term goals and long-term goals.

EXERCISE

What type of leader am I? How well do I embrace the eight mindsets of the customer-focused leader that follow?

FLIP BURGERS AND TAKE OUT TRASH NEXT TO EMPLOYEES.
If you don't, consider taking one day every month to work on the front lines, whether that's literally at your burger restaurant or in the contact center, and take customer questions yourself.

GIVE NO EXCUSES.
Would you consider yourself to be extremely negative or problem focused? Start becoming more aware of how many times

a day you talk about the negative side of a situation, instead of simply taking the steps to solve it.

COMMIT TO EXCELLENCE.

Do you hold yourself to a high standard at work? How do you keep yourself accountable?

SEE FEEDBACK AS A CHANCE FOR GROWTH.

How often do you review feedback from your customers or from your employees? How often do you have skip-level meetings for employees so they can have the chance to speak to their boss's boss?

DON'T TAKE YOURSELF TOO SERIOUSLY.

Are you someone that never smiles? If you don't have any joy in your life, you are not only hurting yourself but the people that need you. Life is too short. Learn how to laugh at times and loosen up. Consider this quote from Joan Rivers: "Life goes by fast. Enjoy it. Calm down. It's all funny!"

BELIEVE EMPLOYEES ARE THE PATH.

If your employees are miserable, your customers will be too. If your employees are joyful, your customers will be joyful.

What do you do to provide an employee experience that is better than average?

KNOW THAT EVERYTHING YOU DO MATTERS.

I like the quote "I only sweat the small stuff" from TV personality and business mogul Bethenny Frankel. If you believed that everything you did in your life mattered a lot, how would you change your lifestyle, how would you treat your colleagues, or how would it affect the decisions you make at work in every aspect?

HAVE A LIFE OUTSIDE OF WORK.

You need a place in your life where you find joy. Often the answer is community. You should not be going to your employees with anything personal, but every human being needs a place to vent and have connection. The more you feed your soul outside of work, the more energy you will have for those who need you.

4

Law 2: Exceed Long-Term Profit Expectations by Focusing on Both Short-Term and Long-Term Profits

It's hard to believe that in 1997 analyst firm Forrester wrote Amazon off as "toast," believing traditional bookstores would destroy Amazon. When their stock plunged, the *Wall Street Journal* ran an article headlined "Amazon.bomb," confident Amazon would fail. From 1998 to early 2000, Amazon raised $2.2 billion, but it was still hard to tell how any of that money was helping make the company profitable. At one point Bezos wrote on a whiteboard, "I am not my stock price," to encourage himself and his team to ignore growing pessimism. He told his teams, "You don't feel 30 percent smarter when the stock goes up by 30 percent, so when the stock goes down you shouldn't feel 30 percent dumber." Bezos notoriously said that he didn't feel the world understood what Amazon was trying to be. But Bezos always knew. He had the ability to withstand being misunderstood by everyone around him.

Who knew he would continue to evolve Amazon into what it is now: continuing to innovate and see the horizon, predicting what the world would need. When Amazon engineers—in the early '00s—were frustrated about the speed of its software engineering, Amazon created a web hosting service that in 2022 made $80 billion in revenue (Amazon Web Services).[1] Increasingly customer-focused companies are less risk averse and more innovative. These companies create more compelling products for customers, have a culture of innovation, and see every problem as an opportunity.

I met Jonathan Adashek, chief communications officer for IBM, at Adobe Summit in 2023 when I supported them by moderating a panel. Later in an interview in the fall of 2023, he shared his own definition of what a customer-focused leader is and about how all too often companies think about only the journey they would prefer for themselves.

"Sometimes people focus on the number—outcome, how much pipeline or revenue—but they lose sight of their clients," said Jonathan. He believes all too often the leader takes the customer on a journey they think is right for themselves, but not for the individual customer. He says people should think about the profile of the individual they're trying to attract.

Jonathan said, "We have to think about how the customer is moving through their experience. Where are the pain points? Where are the opportunities to make different decisions in that journey? Depending on the decision, how do I change what we are offering them, where we are offering it, and the corresponding content?" Jonathan believes that that is fundamental to the success people have in being a client-focused leader. Being a customer-focused company can also mean getting very clear about who you are and what products you want to deliver to customers.

IBM has been through a lot of change in the last fifteen years, in particular the last five. In April 2020, Arvind Krishna, the newly appointed CEO, declared IBM would be the leading AI hybrid cloud company, and just more than eighteen months later spun off Kyndryl, which at the time accounted for one-third of IBM's head count and one-third of its revenue. Jonathan said, "You can't be a 111-year-old technology company without evolving your business and what you offer. That was a $19 billion company with ninety thousand employees, and many people thought, 'You're crazy,' but doing it got us more focused, made us a better company, and helps us deliver on being a client-focused company." Making hard decisions but choosing not to try to be everything to everyone is an important piece of a customer strategy.

Being a customer-focused leader means having the ability to hold two opposing ideas in your mind at the same time, while still retaining the ability to function.

Not giving up on the vision for short-term profits is a matter of priorities. Leaders are tasked with figuring out what to prioritize, and leaders are being judged by what they are doing today, not by the potential of what could happen tomorrow. Leaders feel an immense amount of pressure to generate revenue and reduce costs now, but that can come at a cost to the future. Later in this chapter we look at an example of a business-to-business leader who was tasked with doing both—figuring out how to make money in the short term while also having a vision for the future.

A McKinsey study found that firms that followed long-term strategies amassed $7 billion more in market capitalization between 2001 and 2014 and generated 47 percent more revenue growth and 36 percent more earnings growth, on average, than companies that took a shorter-term approach.[2] But executives still feel immense pressure to create short-term results. One study found that two-thirds of executives and directors reported "pressure for short-term results had increased over the previous five years."[3]

Yet, to succeed, today's modern business cannot be about only profits, and if profits seem too good to be true, they probably are. Later in this chapter we'll look at an example of lack of long-term vision by reviewing Peloton and why the company's valuation took a nosedive.

Short-termism is a real problem for leaders, and it prevents them from making the customer-centric choice every time. Leaders are in a constant state of balancing two pursuits at one time. McKinsey consultants Carolyn Dewar, Scott Keller, and Vikram Malhotra in their book, *CEO Excellence*, state that challenges include "delivering short-term results versus investing in long-term performance. That means taking time to gather facts and do analyses versus moving fast to capture opportunities. How often in the contact center do we stop and say 'what rules do we have for agents that are creating frustrating customer experiences?' There is a lot to think about at one time when you run a customer operation like respecting the past and creating continuity versus disrupting the future. Maximizing value for shareholders versus delivering impact for other stakeholders."[4] F. Scott Fitzgerald once wrote: "The test of a first-rate intelligence is the ability to hold two opposed ideas in the mind at the same time, and still retain the ability to function." This is the essence of the customer-focused leader—this leader is always thinking about what is happening with customers today while also considering all the opportunities for tomorrow.

For example here's a question you could ask: If your industry got completely disrupted overnight, and you could no longer sell what you sell, what would you do?

A study from *Harvard Business Review* reflects that short-termism is negatively correlated with innovativeness, measured as RQ ("research quotient," a measure of the return on R&D investments).[5] Companies with a long-term orientation are rewarded with a lower cost of capital, which allows them to afford more innovation—a virtuous cycle. Profit today is increasingly a reward for long-term focus on disruption and innovation. Leaders today must be able to focus on two things at one time: an eye on what's in front of them now and an eye on what the plan is for the future.

STORYTELLING WITH STYLE: HONEYWELL

When David Cote took charge as CEO of Honeywell International, no one expected him to succeed in turning the company around. He captured his story in his book *Winning Now, Winning Later: How Companies Can Succeed in the Short Term While Investing for the Long Term*. Honeywell is an American publicly traded, multinational conglomerate corporation with a hundred thousand employees. It primarily operates in four areas of business: aerospace, building performance materials, performance materials and technologies, and safety and productivity solutions.

David found that what he called intellectual laziness was endemic at Honeywell. The entire company was gaming the system to meet their numbers each quarter. Executives and managers pursued goals along a single dimension, doing whatever it took to make their numbers in the current quarter without concern for their actions' broader consequences. As a result, Honeywell leaders lacked a clear and honest picture of their businesses and their customers. David was shocked by what he found when he initially looked under the hood. He wrote, "It was all a big mess—short-termism run horribly amuck. I was flabbergasted, pissed, disgusted, and then some. But I wasn't defeated."[6]

He wrote, "Businesses went around in circles, struggling to achieve short-term results and stagnating over the long term." He felt leaders never pushed themselves to develop the kind of new and interesting solutions that would permanently change their businesses for the better and achieve multiple goals at once.

As he embarked on his leadership journey, he found that employees believed you could earn high margins on the goods or services you sold but only at the expense of your sales volume. You could empower frontline employees to make decisions but only at the expense of your ability to maintain control and prevent mishaps. You could improve customer delivery but only at the expense of your inventory reduction efforts.

Great leaders, David came to believe, challenge themselves and others to understand their businesses better and rethink them so that they can achieve two seemingly conflicting things at the same time. He wrote: "That same intellectual discipline—that mind-set of rigor and curiosity—allows leaders to master what is arguably the most important conflict of all: attaining strong short term results while also investing in the future to achieve great long term results."

The short-termism at Honeywell created the opposite of a customer-centric culture: there was a culture of box checking and avoidance of obvious problems. Problems were swept under the rug. The same culture had existed at his prior employer General Electric. He said, "Early in my career, when I worked in various finance and general management positions at General Electric, my colleagues and I were hell-bent on hitting our numbers in the current quarter and year. We'd think about next year, but only when we had to. This obsessive focus on today at the expense of tomorrow didn't make a lot of sense to me. Our business would perform well for most of a given year, and we'd hire a thousand people to help us grow. Then in October and November, we'd create our plans for the coming year, only to realize we'd never make our numbers unless we laid off a thousand people." The decision to hire a thousand people wasn't sustainable and ended up disrupting GE's business and people's lives.

Once David became CEO of Honeywell, the dysfunction around customer experience became clear very quickly. In an interview he told me, "I'll never forget a trip I took early on in my tenure to an air show to visit with a customer of our aerospace unit. The team had briefed me on the visit, and I had gone into the meeting, along with the leader of the business unit, his product manager, and the salesperson, thinking we would discuss a great new product we had. As is my practice, I kicked off the conversation by asking if Honeywell was meeting the customer's expectations. 'I'm glad you stopped by,' the customer CEO said, 'because we have just about finalized the lawsuit we are filing against you for nonperformance on our development project.'" David was shocked and thought, "What?!" His colleagues looked at one another and at David in shock—none of them had known how angry this customer was.

Leaders at Honeywell hadn't studied the customer's operational processes in any depth. They didn't understand the fundamentals of the customer's technologies, their markets, or their business cycles. They didn't know the customer's supply chains. They weren't in touch with how rank-and-file employees viewed the business. They didn't understand key liabilities, such as the environmental lawsuits Honeywell faced. And they didn't understand why their businesses were generating so little cash. David said, "No wonder our company was performing so poorly."

When he came on, no one expected David Cote to succeed and turn Honeywell around. Initially he was torn apart in the business press. As a CEO that no one had faith in, he realized that in order to silence the naysayers he would have to deliver something that quarter while also moving forward with transforming the company and most importantly its culture.

With the pressure on to achieve both a quarterly profit and a long-term strategy win, he realized over time that by taking the right actions to improve operations in the present, Honeywell could position itself to improve performance later. He added that the reverse was also true: short-term results would validate that they were on the right long-term path.

He came up with something called the Three Principles of Short- and Long-Term Performance:

1. Scrub accounting and business practices down to what is real.

2. Invest in the future, but not excessively.

3. Grow while keeping fixed costs constant.

First, Honeywell would address all of their unhealthy accounting and business practices, scrubbing the business down to what was real.

Second, they would courageously sacrifice some earnings today to invest in Honeywell's future, but not too many—they would still take care to do well enough in the short term.

Third, and relatedly, they would become far more disciplined about their operations, challenging themselves to run their businesses more efficiently and effectively so they could keep their fixed costs constant as they grew.

As those improvements and initiatives began to bear fruit, a virtuous cycle took hold: they improved their ability to perform, which would allow them to generate even more cash to invest, which would lead to further performance gains, and so on.

Over the next several years—with David's short- and long-term vision—Honeywell did the seemingly impossible, stabilizing the company and progressing on a number of fronts simultaneously. They tightened up their aggressive accounting, tackled environmental liabilities and other legacy issues, improved their processes and culture, and invested in a range of growth initiatives, including customers, mergers and acquisitions (M&A), research and development (R&D), and globalization. By following these three principles, they forced themselves to consider the long- and short-term implications in every decision they made, instilling cultural and operational norms that allowed the company to deliver more value at all times.

I asked David in our interview what his own customer experience strategy would look like if he took the principles of the overall turnaround and applied them to a customer strategy.

DAVID COTE'S CUSTOMER EXPERIENCE STRATEGY RECOMMENDATIONS

1. **Truly understand what the customer values.** "Be careful you're not hearing what the sales guy says the customer values or what the CEO says or what a consultant's report says, but actually go visit a bunch of customers and just talk to them," David said. He encourages leaders to randomly call fifty customers with a standard questionnaire and ask them questions like, What did they like? What did they not like? Then you will know what the customer values.

2. **Develop metrics that correspond to something that the customer values.** David encourages customer experience leaders to pick metrics that can truly be measured and are robust. "If you measure something, the metric will get better because people learn how to manage the metric. So I was always very careful about any metrics that I put in place." At Honeywell, David didn't have a lot of metrics, but whatever ones he did put in place, he would find a way to audit the metric to make sure that the metric was "absolutely accurate."

David recalled a time when his plant managers were obfuscating the truth when he would ask them about customer delivery. They would say it was pretty perfect. So David decided to do a survey himself. The business leaders protested and said not to do it—that if there were any problems the customers would complain, and they weren't complaining.

As CEO, David did his own customer survey. "I found out it was a serious problem, and customers had either stopped complaining because they got so used to poor performance or customers and frontline employees never raised it up the chain because nobody listened. And we actually had an abysmal performance." He then looked at the plants, and all of them were showing 99 percent customer delivery. What David found shocked him, that the plant managers were excluding anything from the metric they didn't consider their fault. This is an example of how anyone making a metrics analysis can paint the story in a way that makes them look innocent. Being able to audit the metrics is critical.

3. Figure out what the processes are that drive the metric and then process map them (a flow chart that visually describes the process of the work). David said, "Map the process step-by-step and figure out how to create a much more efficient and effective process."

4. Constantly go back and survey again and again. David's own survey he did himself was fifty customers. I call this wash, rinse, repeat. The customer experience work is never done, so the processes you create should be ongoing, constantly investigating:

1. Truly understand what the customer values.

2. Develop metrics that correspond to something that the customer values.

3. Figure out what the processes are that drive the metric and then process map them.

4. Constantly go back and survey again.

Wash, rinse, repeat (see figure 4-1).

Customer Experience Is Wash, Rinse, Repeat

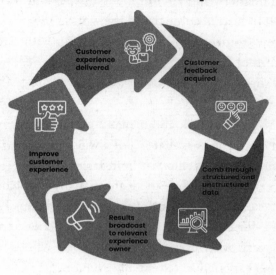

FIGURE 4-1

THERE ARE A few things I didn't know about David until I interviewed him. One was his Boston accent (he hails from nearby New Hampshire). I asked him what his leadership style was, and he said, "I'm decisive, but very thoughtful in arriving in that decision. I think most people would say I have a pretty good sense of humor about things and can laugh at myself and other circumstances. I have a low tolerance and patience for baloney or obfuscation and much prefer somebody to say, 'I don't know,' rather than make stuff up on the spot."

David and his team turned Honeywell into a performance machine, one that satisfied shareholders' quarterly cravings while also becoming much nimbler, more efficient, more innovative, and more customer centric over the long term. From July of 2002 to April 2018, David took a nonperforming company with overwhelming financial and environmental issues and turned it into the leading industrial company in the world. The market capitalization grew from $20 billion to $120 billion with a total shareowner return of about 800 percent, beating the S&P 500 by two and a half times.

LEADERS HAVE TO think about many moving parts in running a company, but the part that is not always as defined or clear is the one with the word *customer* in it. It's easy to forget about the customer's experience when there are so many problems to solve. Customer experience was one of the many problems David Cote had to solve for Honeywell, but customer experience was also affected by every other part of the business. So who is responsible for customer experience? Essentially everyone is!

The problem with customer experience is that the place it most frequently lives is in the contact center. And contact center leaders often do not have the resources to paint the story of why and how much customer experience matters to the bottom line of the business. Only 31 percent of customer experience leaders track the ROI of customer experience. But 37 percent of respondents said they invest significantly to improve the customer experience.[7] The data says that more leaders need to invest in the contact center, and almost 70 percent of practitioners don't know how to track it. Leaders that work on customer programs must make a habit of figuring out ways to connect customer experience to a clear return.

Statistics from HubSpot show an increase in customer retention by 5 percent can lead to a company's profits growing by 25 percent to around 95 percent over a period of time.[8] What are you as a leader doing to track the work your contact center does to retain customers?

STORYTELLING WITH STYLE: SQUARE

Naomi Wheeless is the head of customer success for Square—a financial services platform under Block Inc.—where she manages two thousand people. She was formerly the SVP of operations for Capital One and a call center director at Safelite, both companies known for their customer-centric strategies. Naomi was a key player in Capital One's $9 billion ING acquisition, including product integrations between both companies and marketing campaigns to introduce Capital One to former ING Direct customers. She acknowledged that COVID took a toll on customer experience budgets and believes customer experience budgets have been strained post-COVID.

She told me in an interview, "You need to think about customer experience as a product. As CEOs and boards are looking at the total bucket of money they have to work with, they have to be thoughtful about where they invest."

Naomi believes that experience is the product. Naomi looks at her business the same way Square's product general managers do. She wants to know how many customers her customer success team (agents) are acquiring for Square, and Naomi does this by looking at how many customers call in to Square's phone lines with curiosity about how the software works. She then tracks if the prospect converted after talking to her agent. If you think about it, this makes sense for a financial product like Square where customers enjoy talking to a person to make sure they understand how such an important part of their business—the transaction—works.

Naomi believes her data and analytics around interactions help tell Square's contact center story—how her customer success team is not solely a cost center. She said, "I've invested heavily in all things analytics and data engineering around the profitability customer success brings." And she recognizes if she doesn't actively do this, the value of her customer experience group can be ignored. She acknowledged the value her group brings is invisible unless she calls it out. She said, "I feel responsibility for churn reduction, but it's difficult to tell the narrative in a definitive factual way." According to Gartner, organizations that demonstrate how customer satisfaction is associated with growth, margin, and profitability are more likely to report customer experience success and are 29 percent more likely to secure higher CX budgets.[9]

Naomi's team uses analytics and data science methodologies to do that. She encourages others to have an analytics mindset and tell the customer experience story through hard numbers and not feelings. This will be key to make the case for the requested budget. She encourages others to have a loud voice in the organization and have a seat at the right tables. Naomi said, "Remind them about the importance of caring for the customer's experience. Tell that narrative in a plain way through customer-journey mapping and insights reports." She also encourages people to think of fun and creative ways to get decision-makers to interact with customers and hear the pain points firsthand.

Imagine if you thought of your group like a product team. How would that change how you thought about getting ROI and making the business case? If the experience is the product, a lot of how businesses are run today would be different. Naomi built analytics to be able to tell the story, which is part of making the case for both short-term and long-term strategies.

STORYTELLING WITH STYLE: PROGRESSIVE INSURANCE

There are brave leaders that go right even when everyone else is going left. Tricia Griffith, CEO of Progressive Insurance, is unique, and not just because she has six kids. I'm a mom with two kids and I love interviewing other moms that manage to not only have successful careers but raise amazing kids. I had the chance to interview Tricia about how she quadrupled Progressive's stock price when every other insurance provider was struggling.

She believes in doing things that are not scalable and not measurable. Most business leaders would recoil to hear that, but she understands that when doing the right thing, the ROI is not immediately clear. Tricia, now fifty-eight, started at Progressive in claims at the age of twenty-two, and she would sit across the table from someone who was injured and make snap judgment decisions. She said, "You have to think about how it feels to be the customer," and that's how she settled claims. If she wasn't sure, she would always go with what was best for the insurer or claimant instead of what was most profitable for the customer. Tricia credits her work experience with the lessons she learned in her personal and family life.

She said, "You have to trust your gut." She said she knows how important it is to listen to the customer, because she is well aware of the plain truth about her customer; no customer wants to pay for insurance. She said, "We measure a lot of things, but for many processes we just believe this is the right thing to do."

You would think quadrupling the stock of a company would come from an obsession with measurement, but it came from her down-to-earth leadership style, with which she is a very engaged leader. Her board gives her the room to take risks and gives her the luxury of time to see her programs take shape.

Progressive Insurance is one of the first movers to make the claims process more customer centric and more digital. But it started with Tricia, a CEO that believes in investing in customer experiences you can't always measure or scale. Tricia believes leaders should question everything and make sure they are looking at things differently to understand customers' needs as they change and evolve.

Most companies do not have a CEO like Tricia. Companies are full of well-meaning people that want the company to invest in programs to keep the business healthy for both employees and customers, but they struggle to do that.

Customer experience budgets are generally allocated to the contact center, and whatever way you dice it, when you say, "customer experience," often that is associated with the contact center department. The contact center is the place where customer problems live. While customer experience is the end-to-end experience of the customer, the department that often so badly needs funding and help is the contact center.

IF WE ZOOM out—in the plainest terms—we can also talk about the ROI of putting in effort versus leaving problems unaddressed.

What is the ROI of doing nothing? It's nothing. Matt Watkinson, the author of *The Ten Principles Behind Great Customer Experiences*, told me in an interview he wants people to ask themselves the downside of a customer experience investment. Can you live with an investment in a customer program that doesn't end up creating obvious ROI? If you can then it's a risk worth taking.

Companies today have to constantly reinvent themselves and live in a state of change. Everything is changing around us all the time. Companies have to understand they cannot operate with the mindset that worked during the Industrial Revolution, or even the technology revolution of the '90s and early '00s. Businesses have to understand how to reinvent themselves, and an important piece of reinvention is understanding your company's relevance in the life of the customer. Think back to the example from Honeywell: CEO David Cote expected his team to not just serve the customer but also to take the time to understand the other elements of the customer's business.

If you are living the eight mindsets discussed in chapter 3 (see figure 3-2, page 45), how does this change your appetite for risk and your ability to have a vision as it relates to investments and returns? For example, if you have the energy for influencing change (mindset 1), then you embrace change, take risks, and make a few calculated bets. If you believe employees are the path (mindset 6), then you are willing to invest in technologies and processes that make your employees' lives better. If you give no excuses (mindset 2), then you commit to blocking and tackling the biggest customer problems, and you don't let a mess just sit because it will be expensive to fix. This will cost you later anyway, and companies like Peloton learned that the hard way.

STORYTELLING WITH STYLE: PELOTON

If something seems too good to be true, it probably is. What can be said for individuals can also be said for businesses. If a business has overnight success, there can be problems with the product or with the company's ability to fulfill on the promise to the customer. The pressure on a company to scale overnight can come at a great cost.

There were many small business victims from COVID that did not make it: at least seventy-two thousand restaurants closed during the pandemic.[10] But there were also winners. Any business that created medical products or digital communication products like Zoom or Microsoft Teams or online course companies or digital customer experience technologies boomed, and so did at-home fitness equipment like Peloton. People needed to exercise at home and that was a game changer for Peloton's business. With personalized metrics and engaging content, Peloton attracted a cult following. By November 2020, sales had spiked a whopping 232 percent from the previous year.

Peloton's stock rose 760 percent between mid-March 2020 and mid-January 2021.[11] With that spike in sales, leadership had a hole in its pocket, making quick moves. They bought a $400 million bike factory in Ohio to accommodate the incredible demand from customers,[12] they acquired fitness manufacturer Precor for $400 million,[13] created a clothing line, and almost doubled their employee head count to 6,740 people by June 2021. They spent end-less money to get bikes delivered to customers as fast as possible.

But as vaccines became available and the world opened back up, customers returned to the gym . . . and returned Peloton equipment. Peloton started bleeding cash. Peloton's money had already been spent to accommodate the massive demand for the bikes. Things started to sour for Peloton. Reports surfaced of Peloton injuries from the Tread+ product. In March 2021, Peloton released news that a six-year-old had died after being pulled underneath the treadmill. Peloton still did not recall the treadmill at that time. Peloton received seventy-two reports of adult users, children, pets, or objects being pulled under the rear of the treadmill, including twenty-nine reports of injuries to children.[14] One could assume John Foley, the then CEO, knew that if he were to recall the Tread+, it would be a death wish for the company. All we know is the outcome, which was he denied that there were any issues for two weeks and it made him—and Peloton—look very bad.

One month later, the US Consumer Product Safety Commission warned consumers about the dangers of the popular Peloton Tread+ exercise machine after multiple incidents of small children and a pet being injured beneath the machines, urging consumers not to use it.[15] They did this before Foley had said one word.

That warning prompted a fiery response from Foley, who said the company had "no intention" of recalling the Tread+. This is the worst decision he could have made. He knew that admitting the Tread+ and the Tread were dangerous would hurt Peloton sales. But the right thing to do would have been to acknowledge the problem and send a message to the Peloton community that he was listening and he cared. He chose not to do that. The problem here was not whether it was fair that Peloton got more negative press than other fitness makers that incurred the same problem. Peloton was such a hot brand that everyone was watching Peloton, and when you're seen as a leader, it doesn't matter if accusations are fair or not fair; you have to respond knowing everyone is watching and judging your every move. The customer-focused leader is hyperaware of the optics and makes the ethical decision every time.

Foley later admitted he did not respond quickly enough. He said, "We did make a mistake by not engaging with the Consumer Product Safety Commission in a more productive dialogue earlier in the process." Foley stepped down on September 13, 2022. The recalls happened for Peloton again. In May 2023, two million Peloton bikes were recalled due to a faulty seat. The company's value had fallen from a high of around $50 billion around February 2021 to $3 billion as of August 2023.

If Peloton did not rush to create products so quickly, they could have spent more time thinking through the safety of the treadmill. The CEO would have had more vision—he would have slowed down decision-making to ensure their path forward was sustainable, even if it was slower than everyone wanted. I'm a very loyal customer who still uses Peloton offerings. But even a mostly great product, with highly engaged customers, will not save the company from a lack of foresight and vision. Peloton could have moved slower, even if customers had to wait longer to get their equipment. Had they slowed down, it would have created more of a scarcity buzz around the product. Had Foley been a customer experience futurist, he would have known that the pandemic would eventually end and so would their good fortune of people being forced to work out at home. He could have saved for a rainy day and spent less of Peloton's savings.

It's very possible Peloton knew about these product flaws in advance because they likely came in through the contact center. Usually a product flaw that costs a company millions of dollars starts with one customer calling into the contact center with a concern.

The contact center is a place where potentially very big problems can be flagged. A very two-dimensional view of the contact center is this: the lower the cost of the contact center, the higher the revenue for the company. And while that is true, the contact center can be more than just a cost center but a place where the brand is enriched. The contact center is a magical place, but very rarely do companies see it as that. Many customer leaders tell me they want their contact center agents to be able to upsell and cross-sell to the customer. They want permission from customers to do this, but how much time is spent with these agents to make them feel part of a team? How much are they empowered and trained? The impact your contact center agents have can be directly cor-related with the time you spend on the development and training of these agents.

A BETTER EXAMPLE of how to act in a recall was the strategy of Johnson & Johnson and how they handled the recall of Extra-Strength Tylenol in the '80s. Tylenol was the company's bestselling product back in 1982 (long before social media and the twenty-four-hour news cycle). But in September 1982, seven people in the Chicago area died after taking cyanide-laced capsules. Johnson & Johnson never hesitated. It placed its customers first and quickly recalled thirty-one million bottles (the estimated cost back then was $100 million) and offered replacements free of charge. Then it redesigned the bottle to make it tamperproof.

In 2022, Johnson & Johnson netted a total of $94.9 billion. Recalling the product in a quick and efficient manner did not hurt their brand; it helped their brand. For companies today, the ques-tion is not "will problems arise"—we know the answer is yes. The question is how will you respond when problems inevitably arise, and will those decisions be best for the brand and your relationship with your customer after the dust settles?

When the right approach to customer experience is taken, the board supports the CEO and the leadership team to do the right thing. If you want to look at why an outcome is happening, you have to look at the performance metrics of the people making the decisions. If a leader is judged only by sales for the next quarter, the board cannot expect a long-term view. Almost every action in life can be traced back to what is being measured. How do you gauge success for your team and are you looking at more than just sales and quarterly targets?

FROM CEO TO CX TACTICS

According to a Forrester report, a customer experience "Planning Guide for 2024," CX leaders face difficult investment decisions as they navigate an unprecedented second year of declining customer experience quality, disruption from generative AI, and continued economic headwinds. In today's uncertain economic environment, leaders face more pressure than ever to show the value of their customer programs to the organization. To succeed, they must invest to drive customer-focused action that supports their organization's goals. According to this report, leaders are optimistic about the budgets they'll have as they face these challenges: 64 percent of US customer experience leaders anticipate that their budgets for customer experience initiatives will increase into 2024. Customer expectations are only increasing, and technology has a large role to play. Today 97 percent of brands expect their investment in digital customer engagement to almost double in three years. These investments pay off. For example, in 2023, investment in digital customer engagement increased revenue by 90 percent on average, up from 70 percent the previous year.[16] Customer experience requires constant attention, resources, and investment. The long-term view requires understanding what's relevant for customers today, and where the world is headed tomorrow. As you saw with David Cote, who transformed Honeywell, making both investments for today and for tomorrow can be done. You don't have to choose.

SHORTCUT VERSUS EXTRA MILE

There is always a price to pay for shortcuts, whether that's not investing in proper technology (Southwest Airlines debacle of 2023) or not hiring properly. Examples of short-term versus long-term thinking include hidden fees from wireless providers and cable networks. How about when restaurants slip fees into the bill, like a tip already added in, but don't tell the customer when they sign the bill? We had a contractor on our pool, and we purchased a more expensive pebble for it, but he put in a poorer quality pebble without telling us. Luckily my husband discovered this mismatch by accident. A woman at my dermatology office told me a story about a med spa that knowingly injected elderly female patients with fake products, even though these customers were sold expensive cosmetic treatments.

Do you remember Circuit City? In the '80s Circuit City collapsed under some bad management decision-making. They decided to save some money by firing their more experienced workers who had deep knowledge of their products and replaced them with people that had no experience. Their business folded soon after because of the poor service and expertise they offered customers.

Quiznos, the sandwich franchise, bought the vendors that sold to Quiznos franchises and forced all of the franchises to buy materials only from corporate with a price hike. The margins got way too high, and all of the stores went out of business.

One of the biggest stories of 2023 was about a submarine created by a company called OceanGate that offered customers the ability to explore the *Titanic* at the bottom of the ocean for $250,000 a ticket. It went dark on one of its missions and eventually was found, but nobody survived. After the submersible was discovered, news came out about whistleblowers—concerned about safety— that were silenced. How many stories like this exist where tragedy could have been avoided if only people listened to a whistleblower and didn't have blinders on because they were so clouded by greed or their success?[17]

There is no quick fix or magic bullet to building a successful and sustainable business. Success should be slow and steady. Leaders have to take measured risks, investing in innovation, while not trying to cut corners on their current portfolio of products. Every person today should be thinking about their appetite for delayed success. There is no such thing as overnight success. Most "overnight success" takes at least ten years of slog.

Consider "The Marshmallow Test," an experiment conducted to study delayed gratification in 1972 led by psychologist Walter Mischel, a professor at Stanford University. In this study, a child was offered a choice between one small but immediate reward or two small rewards if they waited for a period of time. In the experiment, the researcher left the child in a room with a single marshmallow for about fifteen minutes and then returned. If they did not eat the marshmallow, the reward was either more marshmallows or pretzel sticks, depending on the child's preference. The researchers continued to track these students and found that the children who were able to wait longer for the preferred rewards tended to have better life outcomes, as measured by SAT scores, academic success, body mass index, and other life measures. While this test seems like a cruel trick, it tells us a lot about success in a time of immediate gratification. Actual freedom and success comes from discipline—because a life or a business with discipline produces better outcomes. Guardrails and rules are a good thing: they keep you on track. What is the board and the executive leadership's appetite for uncertainty?

During times of uncertainty people tend to shrink, to cut costs, and customer programs can quickly get axed. To stay on the long-term road, leaders must have vision.

WHAT DOES IT MEAN TO HAVE VISION?

Salesforce grew from four people to fifty thousand people in twenty-one years. Founder and CEO Marc Benioff creates a one-sheet every year of what he calls V2MOM. This stands for: Vision, Values, Methods, Obstacles, and Measures. Benioff says you have to convince others to align with your vision to plot a course forward. You need to prioritize. And at a big company, you need to scale the process of setting priorities for tens or hundreds of thousands of employees.

"What is the vision for what I want to achieve?"
That's the first question that must be asked, because
if you aren't crystal clear on where you want to go,
good luck trying to get there.
—MARC BENIOFF

His V2MOM includes the following:

Vision—what do you want to achieve?
Values—what's important to you?
Methods—how do you get it?
Obstacles—what is preventing you from being successful?
Measures—how do you know you have it?[18]

At the beginning of each year, Benioff drafts a one-pager detailing his vision, which stays largely steady from year to year while the implementation priorities and methods change. He then gives the document to each of his direct reports and asks them to work with their teams to create a V2MOM document for their own groups. All leaders and their teams are asked to go through all the

V2MOMs to achieve full enterprise-wide alignment and commit to their strategic intent for the next twelve months. Doing this ensures that every unit of the company understands and has agreed to the balance between short-term goals and the longer-term vision in their daily work.[19]

Customer experience leadership that has a vision for long-term profits is done with purpose. There is a deliberate move to say, "This is what we stand for." That requires paying attention to what's happening in society, and not just with your direct industry, employees, or customers.

Benioff is the lighthouse guiding all of his ships. If there is any question about what to prioritize, every ship will go in a different direction. You have to remember what you said you wanted when you embarked on your journey. Benioff and his team say, "Stagnant management tools like once-a-year performance reviews don't cut it in today's fast-moving environment, which requires that companies adapt continuously. Organizations that don't adapt have problems in the long run, and these antiquated tools don't inspire constant change." They believe the V2MOM sparks meaningful dialogue and informs decision-making throughout the year. Employees engage in conversations with their managers around their priorities on an ongoing basis. It's a living, breathing document that can adapt but also stays fixed on the original vision.

EVERY LEADER WOULD BENEFIT FROM CREATING A SHORT- AND LONG-TERM VISION STATEMENT

For too long a focus on short-term profits without thought of long-term implications has caused a lot of problems for employees, customers, and the world in general. We're quickly trying to problem-solve for some major global challenges—including environmental and societal ones—that were swept under the rug for too long.

Again and again the leaders that I interview that succeed with customer experience know that profits can be a little further in the distance when they do the right thing up front and invest in customer experience.

Facing the stress head-on, rather than allowing dysfunction to perpetuate and get worse, makes for a stronger leader and a stronger company.

The leader must focus on the vision and come up with a strategy to protect customer programs from the chopping block. Both good times and bad are an important time to invest in customer experience. It makes sense that when you're making money, and things are up, no one wants to put a wrench in the wheel and slow the company down. But when profits are up, it's a good time to experiment with a new program on a small group of customers (while not spending all of your cash). When profits are down, something is off in how you are providing goods and services to customers. The ability to balance short-term strategies with long-term goals is a key leadership skill today.

The story of the customer-centric leader is the hero's journey. If you ever studied Joseph Campbell, the hero is tested, the hero overcomes adversity, and the hero triumphs over temptation and corruption. There are parallels between the journey of today's modern leader and the hero's journey. In the way companies are set up today, it can feel counterintuitive to make long-term bets. One must be a hero, stronger and smart, and able to overcome short-term distractions and temptations to cut corners.

The customer experience mindset comes in all shapes and sizes, but one thing is clear: the customer experience mindset is a question of character, a question of decisions. It's that saying "The world will ask you who you are, and if you don't know, the world will tell you" by Carl Jung. Or the modern proverb that says, "If you don't stand for something, you will fall for anything."

While Wall Street might be excited by the next shiny object, truly customer-centric cultures often take years, even decades, to build. Being able to focus on the long term shouldn't be a luxury. As you know in your own life, good things take time. There is no such thing as overnight success, for you as an individual or for a brand. True success takes years and years to develop. Relationships also take a long time to build. In your own life you have your ride-or-die people that you can call in the middle of the night when something is wrong. The relationship is built through years of consistently showing up. Becoming a customer-centric leader takes time. To prove you can handle two opposing ideas in your mind at once takes time. You have to prove to your team you can be both short term and long term at the same time. But first that requires you to personally take the time to think through what you're trying to do. Going slow to go fast is something all leaders must consider, however uncomfortable it might feel. And once you build that momentum, nothing can stop you.

EXERCISES

Go through the following exercises to address if your current strategy is short term or long term.

EXERCISE ONE

Take a page out of Marc Benioff's book and answer the following questions:

What is your personal V2MOM? Describe your:
Vision—what do you want to achieve?
Values—what's important to you?

Methods—how do you get it?

Obstacles—what is preventing you from being successful?

Measures—how do you know you have it?

EXERCISE TWO

From David Cote from Honeywell, your short- and long-term strategy questions:

1. Do you understand what the customer values? How will you determine this?

2. What metrics correspond to what the customer values?

3. Figure out what are the processes that drive the metric and then process map them.

4. How often do you go back and survey again and again?

5

---

*Law 3: Lay Out Your Customer
Experience Strategy and Stick to It*

Most times in business there are several
right answers. The leader's job is to pick one.
—JOHN DOERR, CHAIRMAN, KLEINER PERKINS,
Author of *Measure What Matters: How Google, Bono, and the Gates
Foundation Rock the World with OKRs*

If CX is so simple, everyone would do it.

It's much easier to talk about building a customer-centric business than it is to actually build one. Simply put, investing and prioritizing customer experience matters. And while experience centers on relationships and people, it also has a significant impact on the bottom line. Research from Salesforce found that 88 percent of buyers say experience matters as much as a company's products or services.[1]

I meet with leaders from different companies of all sizes, for profit and nonprofit, small and big, and what I've learned is that you cannot simply apply one formula. Creating a customer-centric business strategy looks different at every single company. You can take the same ideas and principles and apply them in different places, but they will look different everywhere you go.

In our personal lives most of us have dreams or fantasies of what we want our lives to be like. We say, "One day I'd like to travel to Greece," or "I really want to lose those fifteen pounds I gained during COVID and can't seem to shake," or "I'd like to find my soulmate," or "I'd like to figure out how I can afford that trip to Disneyland for me and my family." But it's a fleeting thought, and then our mind races on to the next thing as we continue on the hamster wheel of life. The important thing to do for any goal in life is to create a plan to get there.

The hard part is not creating a plan; the hard part is sticking to the plan—and being consistent. It's like exercising—if you don't work out, you lose your muscles. If you want to be in shape, you have to start over every single day and make healthy choices. It's much easier to simply adopt healthy habits so you don't have to think about it; it's just part of your routine. It's the same with being a customer-focused leader. You must constantly go back and fix your recipe to ensure it's always relevant in an ever-changing world. But if you put customer work into your weekly schedule, it will be much easier than if you try and do it randomly.

If your strategy is a wash, rinse, and spin cycle, for a customer experience strategy, that would look like the following (see also figure 5-1):

- **Mission and vision:** Why are you doing what you are doing? How do you know if you've done your job, and what does success look like? Find out what the customer values and what you are capable of delivering to them, and create a vision for your company based on what you find.

- **Create a customer-centric culture:** Culture is not something you can technically see, but the people who work at the company feel it, and the customers are on the receiving end of the culture. In society this can be described as "all the ways of life including arts, beliefs and institutions that are passed down from generation to generation."[2] But the same could be said about companies because often the culture of the founders still exists many years after they are no longer there.

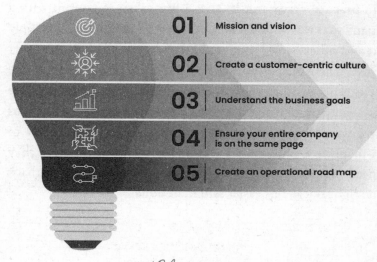

How to Create a Customer Experience Strategy

01 | Mission and vision

02 | Create a customer-centric culture

03 | Understand the business goals

04 | Ensure your entire company is on the same page

05 | Create an operational road map

Blake **MORGAN**

FIGURE 5-I

- **Understand your own business goals** and the intersection of the vision of your customer experience and what outcome you want to drive.

- **Ensure your entire company is on the same page** with your new mission and value set, based on the customer experience outcome you wish to drive.

- **Create an operational road map,** cascade this road map down to all leaders and managers, and ensure that what you are measuring across the company will drive the outcomes you seek.

Every company has a different version of this, but what you generally see is you start with goal setting, then get into how you're going to achieve your goal and figure out a way to keep these priorities in check.

The solution to customer experience is in theory very simple but in practice very hard. In 2023 I was asked to consult with a company that was selling a lot during COVID but due to supply chain and other issues, they could not deliver on their customer promise. Their Net Promoter Score had taken a nosedive. The low customer satisfaction was affecting their brand, as negative reviews rampant online made them seem like a greedy and callous company that just wanted the customer's money. I soon came to learn there were good people working at this company, and they just needed to reorganize around customer experience and get back on the right track. But easier said than done.

Everyone has a plan
until they get punched in the face.
—MIKE TYSON

This Mike Tyson quote was used to describe the reality check I had presented to the customer experience team of a company I had asked to consult for. After two months of working together, in a workshop I delivered some very strong feedback warning them they must aim to do better, with no more excuses.

I am often described as very direct—it is what people like most about me, or dislike about me. This is the style that has always worked for me, but not everyone likes it. I am not cruel, but I believe that if you avoid the truth or lie to someone, you are actually hurting them, especially if you were hired to improve them. If you care about someone, then you will be direct and deliver feedback that is at times unpleasant to hear. This was true of the "trillion dollar coach," Bill Campbell, who many famous people and executives described as a "players' coach." John Doerr, chairman of VC firm Kleiner Perkins and early Google investor, wrote this about Campbell in his book *Measure What Matters*: "You don't know many leaders who convey love and fearless feedback at the same time." You have to be firm but also direct, but it should come from a place of love.

This client's customer experience situation was an emergency. The company had recently been acquired by a customer-centric company in another country, but there was a giant gaping culture mismatch between the two companies.

It took the company an average of forty-four days to close a customer service ticket. It did not have any digital customer relationship management tool or technology to manage contractors that actually executed the work. Everything was done via phone or Excel.

What I found most perplexing was that the culture the company had was in complete contrast to the incredibly customer-focused culture of the parent company, which generated most of their new customers through referrals at a rate of over 90 percent.

Ironically, while the company that acquired this troubled American company was the ideal customer-centric company, they were having trouble imparting their ways on the new company because of cultural differences. All the answers were already sitting in the hands of the parent company. But due to a cultural mismatch and lack of communication and engagement from the leadership of the American company, the parent was raising the badly behaved child who didn't want to listen.

Over a two-month span, I did what a new chief experience officer would do, which included a root cause analysis. In order to figure out where the biggest roadblocks were, I talked to dozens of employees and conducted interviews across the company. I met with lower-level employees frustrated by the lack of upward mobility and opportunity, I met with division presidents who had tons of excuses and didn't believe they had any problems whatsoever, and I met with other executives who were excited by the idea of fresh ideas.

I met with all the leaders, including the newly appointed interim CEO of the company, who I had heard through the grapevine had a brash style—and a few times there were some issues with the language he used in meetings, particularly with the overseas parent company. At one point he said something to the effect of, "If you do not do this, I'm going to put a bullet through your head," as a joke. But the parent company did not think it was very funny.

When I met with him, he vocalized the reasons they had lost sight of the customer, mentioning the stress of production (what was on his plate now) and then on top of that having to think about a customer experience transformation (what was on his plate for tomorrow). Unfortunately for the consulting project, that was the only meeting I had with the CEO. He skipped my in-person customer experience workshop I led that he was slotted to attend.

I provided long- and short-term recommendations.

Major challenges include:

- Leaders who are excellent salespeople but who need to do work on building a customer-centric leadership culture

- Lack of a nationwide standardized approach, with different divisions having different approaches with different resources

- Managing third-party contractors that actually deliver the experience (final product)—communication, say-do ratio, execution, follow-up—while navigating how to overmanage the customer experience when leaders don't have direct management over the process (many layers/complications)

Here were my recommendations to them to get started:

- Leaders must start organizing around customer experience—standardizing—and sharing information across the company instead of competing and being incentivized to compete. You need a collaboration mindset and collaboration software.

- Have an unwavering commitment to quality. Commit to unparalleled craftsmanship and always deliver on the customer promise, every time. You need to agree on quality standards across the company.

- Overmanage the things you care about, and overmanage the production process of the product. You need to come up with a standard way to measure success.

- All decisions should be made through a lens of "what is best for the customer" over what is most profitable in the short term.

- Walk a mile in the customer's shoes, understanding the needs of your customers by always understanding what their preferences are and where the gaps are in what you're providing. Feedback must be gathered and shared with all levels, including leadership, and acted on.

- Customer service should look more like customer success. You need to close tickets faster and more efficiently. You need technology to track that. There is a big accountability gap through the customer journey, from resources allocated for customer service, quality of customer service, and communication to the customer.

- You need to work on creating a culture of humility and positivity in leaders.

- There needs to be better oversight of freelancers and an accountability process for response and resolution rates, and professionalism.

- You must hire a CXO with actual budgetary power / authority / C-level experience.

- You need more diversity in the leadership team.

We together created a new customer experience—North Star—and purpose statement. You can do this exercise with your own team to create a new North Star or mission statement that is more customer centric. Figure 5-2 is an example that I used for our workshop.

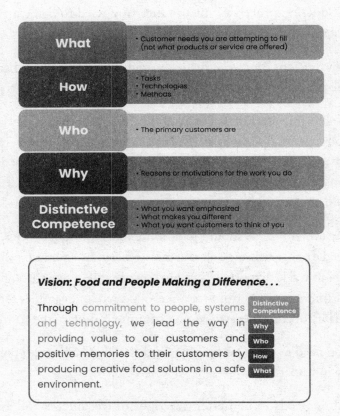

A mindset shift happens when you no longer are consumed with delivering customer service in the cheapest and lowest barrier-to-entry way. A better approach is asking the question, "How effective were we in creating a customer experience we can be proud of?"

We took each goal and broke it down on a timeline—what needed to happen for three months, six months, nine months, and two years. As I write this, I'm happy to report they hired a new head of customer experience and are advancing in their pursuit of becoming a customer-centric company.

EMPLOYEES WILL FIND that, at work, customer experience is extremely hard when the leaders of the business do not embrace it—or believe in it. The entire company will face an uphill battle, always fighting for resources and support, like salmon swimming upstream.

All too often from the inception of an idea, the reason for the company's existence gets lost, and employees are so busy keeping their heads above water that the North Star of why the company was originally founded gets lost.

If people want to buy your product, then you are in the enviable position of being very busy delivering that product. But everyone at times needs to stop and think about the direction of the company and the customer strategy.

The first part of any strategy session is figuring out "Why are we here and what is the outcome we would like to see?" In the last chapter you saw some examples of leaders that have learned to lead with both short-term and long-term objectives. As you prove customer experience is a valuable investment for the business, you will get the support for more investments. You will have your proof points. Again and again we see there is no one-size-fits-all way to create a "customer strategy," and that means something completely different to different people at different companies.

To determine a customer experience strategy, the first question that must be asked is, "What actually is the experience we provide to customers?" You must identify "Where are we now?" "What does success look like?" and "How do we get there?"

Customer experience can be described in its simplest form as a vibe—it is the way you make people feel. But it is also who you provide the product or service to, what you provide to customers, where you provide it, when you provide it, and how it is provided.

STORYTELLING WITH STYLE: MY EXPERIENCE WITH A MENTALIST

My husband and I recently moved to the valley of Los Angeles, California. We attended a show with my in-laws produced by a mentalist. Mentalism is a performing art in which its practitioners, known as mentalists, appear to demonstrate highly developed mental or intuitive abilities. All audience members before entering the auditorium were asked to sign a document saying they were okay with being called on and participating in the show. All of our seats were numbered. When I walked in, I was shocked by how intimate the theater was. I thought there was no hiding from audience participation in here!

The mentalist brought a lot of acting and emotion into his performance to share his colorful past, creating a feeling of mystery and darkness about him. Later in the show he called on audience members and asked them to come to the stage where he would put them on the spot and talk to them. Each audience member was more shocked than the next. The mentalist knew personal details about their lives; it was uncanny! They laughed and they cried. The audience became part of the show. I couldn't believe what I was seeing.

After the show we were driving home with my in-laws, and I sat in wonder. I said out loud, "Wow! How did that guy know all that stuff about those people?" My smart husband nonchalantly said, "That guy has a team that googles each audience member before they attend. The mentalist just studies what information the team finds out online and on social media about each theatergoer before the show. He memorizes it." I was shocked. The guy wasn't a mind reader; he just had a photographic memory. He was very prepared. He knew about each audience member, and it's likely the more the audience member exposed about themselves online, the more likely he was to call on them.

And just as the audience provides breadcrumbs about who they are online, customers also provide breadcrumbs. More often than not, they are inputting information to your company every time they interact with you in person, online, in the app about who they are, where they've been, and what they need. This data can easily feed into a personalization strategy that customers would often prefer as long as it made their life easier and better. Many customers would gladly give up a little privacy for personalization. Accenture surveyed eight thousand consumers from around the world to uncover key data on how consumers feel about personalization. Eighty-three percent said they were willing to share data with brands to receive personalized experiences.[3]

Every company today is like the mentalist. They have the ability with technology to know who their customer is. But many companies are still not yet organized to do this. There is no excuse for making your customer repeat themselves, fill out repetitive information in multiple places, or—the worst—handing them a clipboard of paperwork of any kind when they enter your space. You probably have a very clear image in your mind of the health care office that requires you to fill out a form on a clipboard. And how do you feel when you're handed that clipboard? Probably a little deflated, tired, and annoyed. You know you will be inputting information they already have about you and wondering why they are making you participate in this data charade.

A customer experience strategy looks different at every company, but it starts with an interest in being better. Then it usually involves a spring cleaning of the many messy practices that lead to practices that are not customer centric.

It's not as simple as just deciding to go above and beyond for your customers. The more you dig into companies, the more dysfunction you see. Like one hospital—that my client sold data software to—where departments hoard customer data rather than share it. But some companies have managed to create a culture of a customer experience mindset. They overcome competition and small thinking to create memorable once-in-a-lifetime experiences for customers. You don't have to be a mind reader. For the customer-focused culture, you only need to listen and watch customers. Then you must have a system for putting what you learn into your operations. You must ensure you keep a culture of accountability, and focus and celebrate small, everyday wins. If you do this you won't feel like you have to unravel and rebuild the entire company.

CUSTOMER EXPERIENCE IN FOUR STEPS

I created a simple framework for anyone that doesn't know where to start called W.A.Y.S. (see figure 5-3). I've already shared this framework with thousands of people all over the world, and its simplicity can serve any practitioner that wants to know where to start.

1. **Walk a mile in their shoes.** This means understanding the reality of the customer experience. It means the leader personally goes through the customer journey and knows it inside and out. They feel what the customer feels, see what the customer sees, taste what the customer tastes, and struggle as the customer struggles.

Make Customer Experience a Decision—4 W.A.Y.S.

WALK A MILE IN THEIR SHOES

ASK FOR THE TRUTH

YES TO ACCOUNTABILITY

SMALL IMPROVEMENTS EVERY DAY

Blake MORGAN

FIGURE 5-3

2. **Ask for the truth.** They say the truth will set you free, and that is no truer than in customer experience. Leadership must have a consistent commitment to the truth and always be willing to ask for feedback from employees and customers. The gap between leaders and what's happening on the ground presents a major problem. The wider the gap, the bigger the problem. A customer-centric CEO asks employees to not be intimidated by their title; they want people to be honest with them and to be forward and direct. They constantly seek the truth with data and ask others for help.

3. **Yes to accountability.** Driving accountability is the single hardest thing you will ever do in business. How do you inspire extreme ownership and get every employee to care as much as the person who founded the business? Saying yes to accountability is a mindset. It's the mindset of employees that jump out of bed

in the morning to start their day because they love their work. They love the opportunity to serve their colleagues, their team members, and, of course, their customers. This "jump out of bed in the morning" energy is often innate, but you can inspire it in yourself by shifting your mindset and modeling and inspiring it in your employees.

4. **Small improvements every day.** Overnight success is a myth. Good things take time, and the most valuable experiences take years to build. Business strategy is similar to how you would make a major change in your personal life. You wouldn't do it all at once. Small daily changes have cumulative impacts. It can feel defeating when there is so much to do and you don't know where to start. In the beginning, there is no difference between making a choice that is 1 percent better or worse. But research from *Atomic Experts* author James Clear found that, as time goes on, these small improvements or declines compound and create a very big gap between people who make slightly better decisions on a daily basis and those who don't. It's the same with companies. Companies are only a series of many small decisions made by thousands of people every day. According to research from James Clear, if you get 1 percent better each day for one year, you'll end up thirty-seven times better at the end of one year.[4] Imagine if the whole company starts being just 1 percent more customer centric every day—those compounded efforts mean a lot over time.

IT'S ALL ABOUT experience design and empowering your people to deliver experiences they can be proud of. Giving employees the tools they need to own and deliver great experiences pays off; 82 percent of customers are more loyal to brands that empower contact center agents to solve issues without having to follow a script.[5]

Customer experience requires constant attention. Creating a culture of "fail fast and break things" is critical. Researchers and psychologists have found that overall creativity in US adults is decreasing, largely because of strict work schedules, hyperconnectivity, and a need to always be productive.[6] When employees and leaders are so focused on hitting metrics and checking off tasks, they don't have time to breathe—let alone be creative or have fun. The creativity and the fun can fuel productivity.

Customer experience strategy can be called how you make customers' lives easier and better—or answers the question, "How do you provide value to customers?" When you decide to create a strategy with the customer in mind, you must always look at the anticipated outcome. If we do X, it will affect customers with Y. It might seem like a small mindset shift, but there are huge implications for deciding to be deliberate in how you make decisions.

Consider Chief Technology Officer Ali Bouhouch, who completed the Sephora digital transformation before COVID. He not only had to create a technology strategy, but in order for any of it to work, he had to knock down their current organizational structure.

He said, "We had to change the complete business model, including organization structure, reporting hierarchy, and incentives to stop the competition among channel owners, which, until then, contributed to the fragmentation of the CX and confused our customers."

But when you start digging into the academic research of customer experience, you will find that much of the literature is about creating customer loyalty, or the lifetime value of the customer, which most businesses appear to know. Much less has been written about how to actually create a transaction that makes customers feel good because the focus is on a transaction.

If you do not know where to start on your own strategy journey, you can start with W.A.Y.S. Remember that you also need to create an accountability system to ensure in one, two, five, and ten years the company will not stray from customer-focused decision-making. That is why the approach in W.A.Y.S. should be something that is constantly being conducted. With something as new as customer experience, it helps to create an accountability team or person to ensure that this new customer-centric culture is created and sustained.

STORYTELLING WITH STYLE: KB HOME

KB Home has more than four thousand employees and was started in 1957. Jeff Mezger has been CEO for the last sixteen years. When I meet customer-focused leaders like Jeff, they always seem to just generally be nice people who like other people. They seem to be brought up with values of kindness, integrity, and service. I kept looking for the catch on how a CEO of a new homebuilder could take the giant risk of being customer centric even when the business wasn't making tons of money and the economy was bad. I kept asking him, "How do you explain the quarters of loss to your stakeholders by investing so much in customer experience no matter the economic situation?" I was perplexed by his answers. There was no secret magical equation. He answered simply and said, "Well, being customer-focused is the right thing to do." And even when other firms had supply chain issues that caused delays in move-in dates for customers (and their Net Promoter Scores took a huge hit), KB Home still boasted a customer satisfaction rating of 91 percent. KB Home was ranked the number one customer-ranked national homebuilder and was ranked as one of *Newsweek*'s most trustworthy companies in 2023.[7]

KB Home has six core customer obsession operating principles:

1. Find out what your customers actually want—not what you think they want.

2. Offer choice in everything you do.

3. Customer obsession and innovation go hand in hand.

4. Create collaborative customer relationships.

5. Don't stop listening to your customers when the sale is done.

6. Real customer obsession is a commitment to company culture.

While it might seem trivial, the first step of writing your company's customer-centric mission statement is very important! If what the company actually stands for is not written down, then how will everyone know what the focus of the company actually is?

Again, it's "why are we here and what are we doing here?"

So the bad news is there is no magic formula you can apply and instantly become customer centric. But the better news is, because there is no silver bullet, if you put in the work, you, too, can differentiate on experience, no matter the industry.

Eventually all industries will be disrupted by customer experience leaders, even the ones you can't imagine—like airlines, construction, health care, and internet service.[8] Without the CEO driving, or at least supporting, I do not believe customer initiatives will be successful.

A company does not need to appoint a chief customer officer or chief experience officer to create a customer-focused environment. Anyone can be a customer-focused leader, should they *decide* to do so.

The important thing to remember is that mindset is a decision, but it's also backed by physical moves. With that increased focus, how can you design processes and governance internally that improve the customer experience? There's been a massive digital disruption in the last few years changing almost every aspect of your business.

STORYTELLING WITH STYLE: THE BEAR

The show *The Bear* on FX (and Hulu) is a story about a young chef from the fine dining world (named Carmy) who comes home to Chicago to run his family's sandwich shop after his brother commits suicide. It's a far cry from his former job at a Michelin star restaurant and life in New York City, and Carmy must balance the soul-crushing realities of small business ownership, his quirky and accident-prone kitchen staff, and his strained personal relationships with his family, while processing his brother's death. The show captures how Carmy fights to transform both the shop and himself. He works alongside a rough-around-the-edges kitchen crew that ultimately reveals itself as his chosen family.[9] In season two his co-worker Sydney, in the face of all she's seen, still wants to win The Bear (restaurant) a Michelin star, and Carmy warns her of the cost: "You're going to have to care about everything more than anything."

This is the heart of a customer-centric company. Everything is your business! True ownership is when you care deeply about even the most subtle details. Being a customer-centric company is like having a Michelin star, but no one awards you with it in this scenario. You have to set your goal and decide how you will get there. And no two companies are alike. Hospitality has some of the best use cases on customer experience because there is no hiding bad service. Good service is the cornerstone of the world's top airlines, hotels, and restaurants.

There are so many business books and articles that talk about the very clear-cut value of the world of customer management. But customer experience is more than the channels you talk to customers on and the metrics you use to measure how that's going. Customer experience is the end-to-end art of business.

You have to create a culture of caring with the same kind of intensity and gusto you would see in a Michelin star kitchen. In the kitchen of a nice restaurant, there is a clear order. Everyone in unison must say "Yes, chef" when the chef or leader gives direction. In the very chaotic art of fine dining, and making a meal an experience, when every detail is scrutinized, there is no room for error. Before we even dive into creating a customer experience strategy, we must ask the question, "Do we have a culture of caring about everything?" So one must ask the question, "Is work and life better when we care about everything?"

The companies without a customer experience strategy will eventually have to redo all the broken experiences they've delivered, and they will pay for them. In 2022, Sitecore found that poor customer experience cost businesses in North America more than $200 billion annually.[10] While if we care deeply, and we think about every potential scenario, and we plan as much as we can to avoid any employee or customer stress, we make much more money in the long run. Caring more up front is a strategy, and it saves you from having to backpedal, which not only costs you money but costs you in stress, broken trust, and damaged relationships at work with your employees and with your customers. Having a customer strategy is the vision we talked about in chapters 2 and 4. Without a lighthouse to direct your ship, short-term emergencies can veer you off track. A leader needs to put a stake in the ground and say, "This is important to us."

In this chapter I shared with you my own consulting work as a customer strategist and how you, too, can simply decide to be the change agent within your company and begin to sketch out a blueprint of where your company is and where you need to be. No two strategies look the same. It's important for you to stay in your own lane and figure out what will make your own company successful, without getting extremely bogged down in what your competitor is doing. In the next chapter we're going to take a look at what you can do in your first ninety days.

EXERCISE

Make your own customer experience strategy by working through the following questions.

Mission and Vision: Do you have a mission and vision and are they customer-focused? When was the last time you rewrote them?

Create a customer-centric culture: Do employees like working at your organization? Do they feel proud to work there? Would they recommend working at your company to their friends and family? Do they have what they need to do their job?

Understand your own business goals: What behaviors do your business goals drive? Are they in line with your mission and values?

Ensure your entire company is on the same page: Do teams in your organization collaborate around the customer—or do they compete?

Create an operational road map: Have you created a road map and shared it with other key leaders in the organization? Do you have the support to make it happen and are others excited to bring the customer experience strategy to life?

Answer these questions with your teams:

What makes your product or experience unique and what are the areas to differentiate on?

How can you reduce stress for customers?

What are your top three customer offenders (what do customers hate about doing business with you)?

What makes customers want to come back and tell their friends?

Do you have someone who can—at the leadership level—be accountable for your customer experience transformation?

If you are not the CEO, do you have the CEO's support?

What is the cultural transformation that needs to happen to ensure you move in the right direction?

How will you create a culture of continuous feedback and distribute that across the company?

What are you doing to invest in the contact center and develop these customer-facing agents?

How can you help marketing, sales, and service collaborate more?

What incentives are you giving employees, and do they drive the right outcomes?

6

Law 4: Embark on Your Ninety-Day Get-Started Plan

Pressure is a privilege.
—BILLIE JEAN KING

It's important, when you start a new role, that you start strong. Monday kicks off the pace for the entire week. Many of you reading this are building your own job description: you are the first person to be the chief customer officer or perhaps your role doesn't even have a title yet. Beginnings matter a great deal. First impressions matter, and when you start a new role everything you do is being watched and judged. That's why it is absolutely critical to make the right first impression immediately. At the same time, you need to be figuring out how you will be successful in your new role to make your organization more customer centric.

The more experience you have leading customer strategy programs, the easier your jobs will be when you "start over." But every new role and every new company will feel challenging. Even though the beginning is challenging, you cannot lose your focus or your cool. It is important that early on you create a reputation of being a fair, dependable, and ethical person. Take your values with you into your new role because everyone will be evaluating you in those first few months. Be careful about what you say and what you do. Listen more than you talk.

Leadership is only about influence and leverage. These two things you will build over time. You need influence to get things accomplished. Leverage is the ability to influence situations or people so that you can control what happens.[1]

You might have a new role with the word *customer* in it, or perhaps not. Either way, if you picked up this book, you are hungry to create a better world. You have the power to effect change at work.

LEADERS IN TRANSITION

In a new role, leaders feel the pre-beginning jitters, and that's totally normal. Leaders can feel nervous, just like all employees. But they are not supposed to show it! Make sure that you leave room to deal with your own anxieties. While not everyone can do these things, I encourage you to, if you can, get up early so you can meditate, exercise, have breakfast with your kids, play with your dog, listen to music in the shower—do whatever you have to do to keep your mind calm and clear.

The customer leadership role is tough, because you are walking into an uncertain situation where you will need to be an investigator. At times you will feel like you're at a start-up because the path is not clear. You will need to build the airplane as you fly it.

---

*The best advice I have for you is this:
don't run away from stress; run toward it.*

Phil Stutz, famous psychiatrist to the stars, recommends you should tell yourself the mantra "I love pain." These reverse psychology tactics help to diffuse the stress of doing things that are uncomfortable. No matter what you do before you start your workday, you should ensure it leaves you feeling energetic, focused, and happy.

Going toward stress and pain is a life and work strategy. Many problems happen in life because human beings avoid pain and stress. Stress and pain actually challenge us to step up, to be the best version of ourselves. If they run toward stress, individuals are much more successful than if they avoid it. Why am I writing about stress? Well, customer roles are stressful enough, but starting a new job can be very challenging. Maintaining a healthy state of mind is critical. I interviewed Oscar Munoz, who had a heart attack just thirty-seven days into his new job as CEO of United. He had spent the first month flying around the world meeting as many United employees as possible, flying through time zones and trying to get acquainted with the world of United, which was in a very bad spot. He was vegan, didn't drink coffee or alcohol, and didn't smoke. But he still had a heart attack. Your first job, before you even show up at work, is to do whatever you have to do to get yourself into a calm, cool, and collected headspace.

Some of the goals you will need for yourself in your new role include achieving early wins for credibility, finding advocates and building relationships, making informed strategy decisions, and finding focused learning time (you have a learning curve) while not drinking from the fire hose and getting overwhelmed.

Your job is going to be challenging because you have two tasks to take on:

1. Create a customer-focused strategy or grow and improve what is already there.

2. Get the highest performance possible from your team—because you are ultimately a coach.

The role of the customer-focused leader is to make life better for employees and customers. Your job is to effect change—starting where you can and spurring innovation. Ultimately you want to create a customer-focused culture across the company. What does that look like? The culture would be affected by employee-feedback programs, customer-feedback programs, metrics that are driving customer-focused behavior across the company, and a constant focus to reduce back-end complexity.

A culture of politics and ego will destroy the pursuit of customer experience.

While challenging the status quo is important, you also need to take a measured approach. I once had a boss whom I respected and liked; but one day he got so mad he threw his computer. Not long after this incident he was fired, not because of this incident in particular, but because he could not control his emotions and could not play the game that was required to work at this company. He could not get the rest of the organization to like him, and he did not build camaraderie. If you blow through an organization like wildfire, with no strategy, you will not be successful in achieving the change you seek.

The first ninety days you should not be the loudest person in the room, and you will need to craft your strategy partially based on your rank and role. While you should feel comfortable challenging processes that don't make sense, you also need to be a good listener, figuring out how things work. From a customer experience perspective, your leadership role needs to be about creating a new customer-centric vision, identifying the gaps, and then figuring out how to mend those gaps.

What made you successful in the past will likely not apply to what will work for you today, so don't live in the past. The more success you achieve early on, the more resources and advocacy you will have to keep going, and the more results you bring, the more respect you will garner. Michael Watkins, in his internationally bestselling book *The First 90 Days: Proven Strategies for Getting Up to Speed Faster and Smarter*, gives great advice for leaders in new roles. His advice on your first three months on the job is relevant to a customer leadership role as well. I've taken his advice and applied it to the customer strategy world. Figure 6-1 was inspired by Michael Watkins, detailing the first ten goals in your customer experience role.

Customer Experience Role

Inspired by Michael Watkins of *The First 90 Days*

CX listening tour	**01**	**06**	Achieve CX alignment	
Gain tools for rapid learning	**02**	**07**	Build your CX team	
Match CX strategy to each situation	**03**	**08**	Create CX coalitions	
Secure early CX wins	**04**	**09**	Ensure you are not overly stressed	
Negotiate CX success	**05**	**10**	A rising tide lifts all boats	

Blake MORGAN

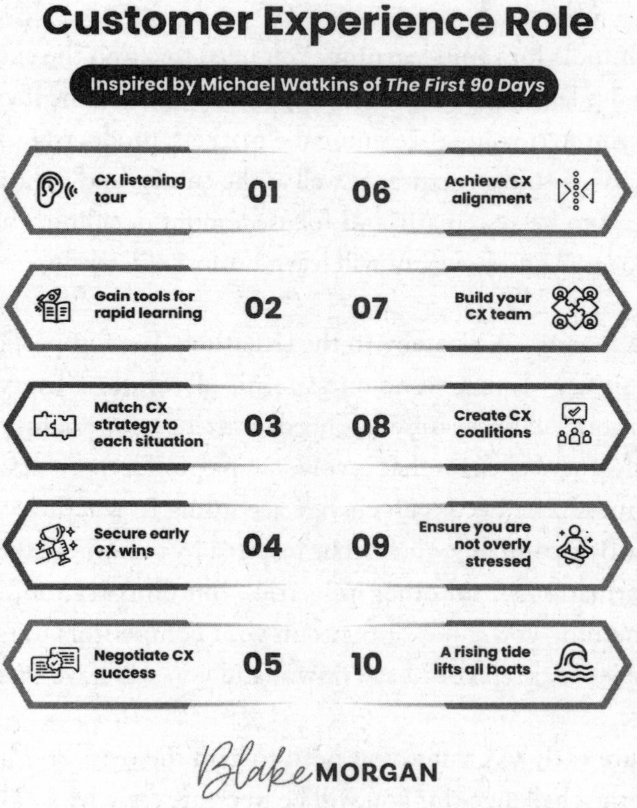

FIGURE 6-1

Your First Ninety Days in Ten Steps

1. Go on a CX listening tour. I remember when I interviewed Ali Bouhouch, the CTO of Sephora who I mentioned earlier, who launched a complete digital transformation of the company that was extremely successful. I asked him what he did in his first ninety days, and I was surprised he told me he went on a listening tour. He simply met with different business units and employees to learn what their pain points were, and he hardly talked for the first six months. Amy Shore, chief customer officer at Nationwide, did the same. Getting started is about **soaking** it all up and figuring out how an organization works.

2. Gain tools for rapid learning. You need to climb the customer experience learning curve as fast as you can. Spend time if you can before you start your job learning the markets, products, technologies, systems, and structures as well as the culture and politics. You will need to be systematic and focused about deciding what you need to learn and how you will learn it most efficiently.

3. Match your CX strategy to the situation. The fun part of customer strategy is there is no one-size-fits-all solution. Everywhere you go you will find a different need. Start-ups, for example, present different challenges that involve a new product, process, plant, or business. The needs can change according to whether you're a B2C or B2B company. You can be inspired by customer experience transformations from other industries, but don't try too hard to be something you're not or focus on your competitors too much. Do the work, keep your head down, and you will have success.

4. Secure early CX wins. You need to gain the trust of others, so one of the challenges for you will be to create early wins. This will build your credibility and create momentum. Michael Watkins calls this a pattern of "virtuous cycles." Successful customer experience projects will create improved products, happier employees, and you will have an easier time securing more investment for your customer programs. It's important to create value and improve business results that will help you get to the break-even point faster. The break-even point is when in your transition you have contributed as much value to the new organization as you have consumed from it. When more than two hundred CEOs and presidents were asked for their best estimates of the time it takes a midlevel leader who has been promoted or hired from the outside to reach the break-even point, the average of their responses was 6.2 months.[2]

You might come across some programs that are very positive that you don't need to create from scratch. Be careful that you don't have the "not-invented-here-syndrome." This is a tendency for people to avoid things that they didn't create themselves. This can be the result of pride that makes an organization believe that it can solve a problem in a better way than preexisting solutions already do. Pride isn't the only contributing factor that triggers it; jealousy can also play a role.

5. Negotiate CX success. Figure out how to build a working relationship with your new boss (or many bosses) and manage their expectations. This is the most important relationship you have in the organization. This means plan for a series of critical conversations about your situation, expectations, working style, resources, and your personal development. You also need to agree on your ninety-day plan with your boss.

6. Achieve CX alignment. The higher you are in the organization, the more you must play a role of organizational architecture expert. To achieve alignment you have to figure out the business's strategic direction and make sure every business unit is dancing the same dance. If you launch a customer experience program in a corner of the organization and don't collaborate with any other group or tell anyone else, you're not going to be successful.

7. Build your CX team. One of the best pieces of business advice I've received was given to me recently by customer experience consultant and small business owner Allen Dib in an interview. When I asked him what his best business advice would be that helped him achieve great success, he said, "I don't tolerate anything but an A-player."

That said, if you want to have a team of A-players, you have to be an A-player yourself. While it can seem hard to make these sweeping changes, once you do, and you find good people, the results are fairly immediate. Low performers who don't appreciate the work can feel like dead weight, bringing down the performance of the entire team. People that are negative, that are sarcastic and angry, or put down others—these are bad apples that must be weeded out. People who say "that's not my job" are the antithesis of the essence of the customer experience mindset. The people you find when you build your team don't have to be perfect, but they must be coachable and put their heart into their work.

8. Create CX coalitions. Your success depends on your ability to make an impression on others and get them excited about the work you're doing and help them understand their role and how they contribute. This is your time to inspire advocacy and find pockets of the organization to rally around your programs. These are people who can be the spirit of the customer in the room wherever they go and help drive awareness of what you're trying to achieve.

9. Ensure you are not overly stressed and aim for balance. Maintain equilibrium and balance. Accelerate your personal transition and gain more control over your work environment. Carol Carpenter, the then CMO of VMware, told me in an interview that she had a "kitchen cabinet" and that has helped her in life and work. It is a group of various people she could always go to for advice and support. Even leaders need coaches, and even leaders need support systems and community.

10. Be the tide that raises all boats. You are going to have to be a salesperson for customer experience. If you can understand what motivates others, you will have an easier time creating common denominators that everyone can get behind. The more you understand the other players, the faster you will be able to help them see that a customer-focused business will make everyone more successful. It is your job to make everyone successful, and by making others successful you will create a good reputation—as someone who brings results and cares about others.

NOW THAT YOU'VE seen this ten-step plan, you can think of a more specific plan for yourself, and you can break it down into chunks. What will help you operate in a compressed time frame?

STORYTELLING WITH STYLE: US WOMEN'S SOCCER COACH JILL ELLIS

Jill Ellis, a coach inducted into the National Soccer Hall of Fame, learned how to be a soccer coach from her dad, who was also a coach. When she fell in love with soccer, there were no women playing soccer in the UK where she lived. In the Netflix documentary *The Playbook: A Coach's Rules for Life*, Jill talks about the mindset of the competitor: "You should have the mindset you have something to prove even if you're the best in the world." When Jill took over the US women's national team in 2014, it had been fifteen years since they won the World Cup. They had some early success and won the World Cup in 2015, but in 2016 something went very wrong. In the quarterfinals they lost to Sweden in penalty kicks. It was a devastating upset. They finished the worst they had ever finished in a world event. The news reverberated around the world about this upset. It was a wake-up call for Jill, who says there is no lesson greater than losing.

She said, "Success is never resting on your laurels, because someone is always gunning for your spot." She knew that Sweden's defeat of the US was going to be a blueprint for other teams.

She was disappointed and frustrated and knew she needed to act quickly. Sweden had a smart strategy to win the game. Sweden's team eliminated the space of the US soccer players on the field, compacted their team, and sat lower on the field, making the US team's space hard to find and hard to take advantage of (the US could not score a goal). The US needed something they did not have. They needed a new type of player that could move around the field differently.

Knowing this would be controversial, Coach Jill decided to go for a hard reboot. She said, "This failure is now an opportunity for us to explore, find new players, and add to the depth. It's going to be uncomfortable, hard, and stressful. But I need you to buy into this process."

Jill cut people everywhere, lowered players' contracts, and left players off the rosters. It was a massacre. She changed almost everything. It was a very hard period for Jill and the entire team, a period of transition. The press lambasted her, fans called for her firing, and her two team captains confronted her. The players were frustrated by all the changes. Her job was on the line and rumors of her being fired circulated. But Jill stood her ground and said, "I'm not coaching to keep my job. I'm coaching what I believe."

Coach Jill said, "You can't get into leadership if you're always pandering to the critics or even your employees. You have to have a sense of self that you are doing what you believe. . . . The storm was raging. I had to keep the belief and the faith in myself." Finally, at a tournament of nations in 2018, the tide started to change. The game didn't start off pretty for the US; Brazil scored first off the foot of an American player who accidentally scored for the other team. But finally during the game the team started to operate in synchrony. Her strategy on spacing and skills worked! The US beat Brazil 4–1 and won the entire tournament. And that was the beginning of a new era of women's soccer led by Jill. With continuous superstar performances, the team won the World Cup again in 2019.

In 2019, Jill's team didn't just play soccer; they managed to spark a worldwide discussion of equal pay for women athletes leading into the women's World Cup. Their guiding light and motivation was their drive to make a statement about fair pay. They sent shock waves around the world by making a statement and giving the bold sports performance to match it by winning the World Cup.

HOLD FAST, STAY TRUE

Something I learned from Coach Jill was her respect for the Navy SEAL mentality. When the SEALs go into tough situations their mantra is "Hold fast, stay true." When a storm rages and waves lash, the sailors have to hold something that's connected and tied down to the deck. The person at the wheel has to stay true to the direction, even though they can't see the stars because of the storm. Hold fast, stay true. "Customer work" generally involves an amount of uncertainty and constant innovation; the work is never done because things are dynamic, fluid, always changing. And what was relevant yesterday is not relevant tomorrow in the life of the rapidly evolving customer.

It's normal that in your first ninety days there will be some huge waves that throw you off your game or make the journey feel very uncertain. The key is to stay the course, hold on to what you can, and don't lose faith in yourself and the important work you are doing.

EXERCISE

As you start your new role, how will you achieve the following?

GOALS TO ACHIEVE IN YOUR FIRST NINETY DAYS

A message from the CEO

A preface about why the company needs the customer experience strategy

Vision statement

A list of the strategic focus areas

A description of your customers

Quantitative and qualitative measures

A customer service charter

An action plan—short term and long term

PATH TO GET THERE

1. Go on a listening tour.

2. Accelerate your learning (learning curve).

3. Match your strategy to the situation.

4. Secure early wins.

5. Negotiate success.

6. Achieve alignment.

7. Build your team.

8. Create coalitions.

9. Ensure you are not overly stressed and aim for balance.

10. Be the tide that raises all boats.

7

Law 5: Anticipate the Future:
Be a Customer Experience Futurist

The average life span of an S&P 500 company has fallen by 80 percent in the last eighty years (from sixty-seven to fifteen years), and 76 percent of companies in the FTSE 100 companies have disappeared in the last thirty years.[1]

If you go back fifty years and look at the balance sheet of Fortune 500 corporations in the 1970s, what you find is that more than 80 percent of the value came from physical stuff. According to Alan Murray, CEO of *Fortune*, these are products that required investment to support equipment, oil in the ground, or inventories on the shelves. So it makes sense that businesses back then focused on returns on capital and on financial returns to shareholders. But if you do that same exercise today, what you find is that more than 85 percent of the value of the Fortune 500 is in intellectual property, software, and brand value—meaning the emotional connection that a brand has with customers. These are "intangibles" that are much less physical but are also much less dependent on financial capital and much more dependent on people—on human emotion and human ingenuity, the creative and resourceful capacity of human beings to come up with innovative solutions, ideas, and inventions to address challenges and improve various aspects of life. There is a trend among businesses (including Fortune 500 companies) to focus less on selling physical products and more on providing services, experiences, and software.[2]

Thanks to the digital explosion of the early 2000s, almost everything about what businesses sell has changed or been affected in some way. Companies might focus more on selling *access* to platforms or ecosystems rather than *individual products*. Apple sells hardware like iPhones and MacBooks, but a lot of its revenue comes from its ecosystem of services like the App Store, iCloud, Apple Music, and Apple TV+. Companies like Google, Meta, and many financial institutions primarily deal in services, data, and digital products rather than physical goods.

Businesses are operating in a world where increasingly the products being sold are not physical products at all. One of these intangibles is the relationship the customer has with the brand. This can be likened to a relationship you might have with a neighbor that constantly helps you out. When you have a relationship with a customer based on trust, that's an intangible too.

Increasingly the value of a company is not what it used to be—the value of a company is its ingenuity, its relationships, and its psychological power in the customer's mind.

WHAT IS A FUTURIST?

There were signs that the future would be much more customer-focused, and more digital, but not many predicted the extent to which customers' lives would be affected by technology or the attention that would be paid to anything with the word *customer* in it. While some industries have ebbed and flowed, the customer experience software industry—and related businesses—have grown exponentially. If the product is no longer the differentiator, and the service around the product is, what is the role technology will play in that? And at what point will customers get fed up with technology and yearn for more human interactions? The balance will be very important for businesses to figure out.

A *futurist* is a person that systematically explores predictions and possibilities about the future and how they can emerge from the present.

A *customer experience* futurist considers the business implications of the broader trends and changes in society and how that could affect your customer base. Today's technology landscape presents the fastest, deepest, most consequential disruption in history, and society is still in limbo in understanding and accepting what that means for us. In the next ten years, five foundational sectors—information, energy, food, transportation, and materials—that underpin our global economy will incur immense change.[3] Thanks to technology, costs will fall by more than ten times, while production will become much more efficient, using 90 percent fewer natural resources and producing ten to a hundred times less waste. You're seeing more innovation than society has ever encountered, coupled with more uncertainty than ever before on a variety of fronts. The world needs leaders that understand futurism and think about it all the time.

Questions and curiosity should always be top of mind for leaders, such as:

- What are tangentially related market players to your business?

- What is going on in the world in relation to the production of your product?

- What about the changing tastes of customers?

- Or new technology inventions?

- Or implications for your business from the world's changing environment?

- What does the next generation of customers want from a product or service? How do they prefer to engage with a brand?

- Is our brand message still relevant for today's buyer?

In both your personal life and in business you need to manage today's load, but you also need to keep your eye on the future. It's the job of balancing two pursuits at one time. Getting out in front of those changes is a leadership advantage. There are usually signs that something will come along that will affect you and disrupt the equilibrium. Sometimes attention and investments are necessary even when the board doesn't understand the clear ROI. In 2022, JPMorgan invested $12 billion in digital transformation. Jamie Dimon, the CEO, said he wanted to do two things with this money: run the bank and change the bank. Analysts pushed back on Jamie's decision, and his style was described as defensive. Jamie Dimon was tough with analysts who wanted more clarity and specifics on the firm's expanding tech spending, including an understanding of when the firm expected these investments to yield profits. Jamie said, "A lot of you want payback tomorrow and stuff like that. We'll not disclose those numbers, but we are there for the long run. We're going to be adding products and services and countries for the rest of our lives. So I doubt, over the long run, we'll fail." It was not a popular announcement, but Jamie knew he was doing the right thing.

Like Jamie, you must always hold two diametrically opposed ideas in your mind at one time: take care of what is in front of you today while also always thinking about and investing in tomorrow.

Being a leader today means being not just comfortable with uncertainty but being prepared for all scenarios—and also looking at the past to predict the future. COVID exposed that the world was not well prepared for an unpredictable event. People did the best they could, but governments, employers, and health organizations could have handled COVID better and have been better prepared. COVID was a reminder for every business that you need to be ready for anything, ready to turn on a dime.

When something comes out of left field, most societies do not have the resources or leadership to combat it easily.

CUSTOMER EXPERIENCE FUTURISM

The biggest three areas that are likely to evolve are customers' expectations of the brand, what the brand sells, and how technology will affect the delivery of the experience.

The incoming generation often drives change, and older generations adapt to the changes driven by the younger generations.[4] As smartphone natives, Gen Zers have high expectations; they've had technology and smartphones since they were born. Gen Z is only 50 percent satisfied with current customer experiences compared to 71–72 percent for previous generations.

Gen Z is savvy at manipulating and conditioning algorithms to dictate their lives online. They know everything they click shapes their experience online. By doing this they're also wrestling the control away from platforms that are trying to collect their information. So the values we see becoming more important for this generation than for others are purpose, control, and individuality.

Recent research indicates that 15 percent of audiences don't report a strong commitment to a familiar brand. In contrast, a strong brand commitment means a high brand connection, preference, advocacy, and willingness to pay more or a premium for a brand. But those experiences are few and far between. Customer loyalty is created by experiences that are emotional and have a personal impact on customers' lives, according to Gartner.[5] A unique customer experience has double the impact on brand commitment.

Brands need to figure out where the customer's emotional needs live within the customer experience. After step one, brands must adapt to their needs and provide them with a digital-first customer experience that identifies opportunities to pepper in a personal touch.

Recent research from Experience Dynamic reports that 53 percent of Gen Zers say an interaction/experience that leaves them feeling worse causes them to remember a bad experience.[6] Gen Z is more forgiving after a bad experience as compared to older generations. They're willing to give companies 2.6 chances to make up for a bad experience as opposed to the 1.1 chances that boomers are willing to give.

All of this research illustrates that the customer experience of the future requires operating models that bring together teams that have classically not collaborated around the customer.

HOW CUSTOMER EXPERIENCE WILL BE AFFECTED BY AI

If you want to be a futurist, you can't just focus on what customers will buy in the future; you have to understand how life on Earth is evolving and the role you and your company plays in that dynamic reality. Artificial intelligence is a discussion that is more science fiction than what we're used to. OpenAI's research estimates that 80 percent of today's workers could see their jobs affected by generative AI.

The market for artificial intelligence is set to hit $1.8 trillion by 2030.[7] In 2022 the global market size was valued at US$136.55 billion. Generative artificial intelligence—data-trained technology that uses prompts to create content—saw a massive uptick in adoption in 2023.[8] The technology has advanced significantly within a short time frame, and relatively speaking, it's just getting started.

Kevin Surace, a technology leader with one hundred patents, thinks humans will not be replaced with AI for many decades. He said, "While the human brain in total will not be replaced with AI in the next few decades, virtually none of us use our entire brain for our job tasks. More like 10 percent or 20 percent. Think about it. Most jobs simply have never required 100 percent of one's mind. So envisioning that AI and robots to replace 10 percent of one's brain, especially in more repetitive tasks, seems plausible."[9] There is so much complexity in most operations today. AI could help that. Every company today should be in a race to simplify and reduce friction for both employees and customers. I made a presentation for the senior leadership team of AT&T, and one of the ideas we talked about was the importance of reducing back-end complexity. Every company today needs to have this on their board agenda.

The exponential growth of AI has created many ethical gray areas and watchdogs calling to slow down the speed of AI development. One of the biggest opportunities and fastest adoption rates is in customer service. Although Goldman Sachs says AI could replace the equivalent of three hundred million full-time jobs,[10] most experts agree that customer service jobs will be augmented and automated but not replaced. By automating mundane tasks, AI could provide a better experience for customers with more self-service options and help fix some of the industry's biggest problems, especially employee burnout and inefficiency. Even if AI does replace customer service agents, there is still a role for humans— and that is to focus on the hospitality of the customer. Working in customer service is notoriously stressful—it was named one of the world's top ten most stressful jobs—and companies see turnover rates of up to 45 percent of agents every year.[11] AI could offset the all-too-often terrible employee experience of working in a contact center. Such experiences have led to a massive talent shortage and makes it costly for companies, which have to continually recruit and train new employees—all of which affects the customer and employee experience. AI won't replace human customer service jobs in the short term simply because there are so many open jobs.

With limited budgets and talent shortages, contact centers are looking to do more with less and make the most of their limited workforce. AI is the best tool for both of those issues.

As I mentioned, many are wondering if AI will replace workers. Daniel Hong, former Forrester analyst and current CMO of Minerva, an artificial intelligence start-up focused on reducing call times in the contact center, likens AI in the contact center to navigation apps and how they are helpful for drivers. Many like Daniel predict AI will supplement work, not replace it. He calls AI technologies "Waze for agents."

When I was in the Philippines, I spoke to a room of C-level executives for Globe, one of the biggest technology and telecom companies in Southeast Asia. A consultant in the region, Josiah Go, who is also a director at the UnionBank of the Philippines, warned the room about being disrupted. Contact centers are a major export of the Philippines, and he said, "Beware of AI— in particular emotionally intelligent AI—because what will our role be then?" Contact center agents have started training the AI that could supplement their jobs. For example, Teleperformance's 410,000 employees are training Microsoft's AI platform called Azure Cognitive Services. The partnership takes data from the Teleperformance contact center team's interactions, including both audio and digital conversations. This creates business insights and drives enhancements, including a chatbot that helps Teleperformance agents resolve customer requests faster and more accurately.[12] And last, real-time translation services for a hundred languages enables customer care experts to respond in any language, and do so faster and more accurately.

Microsoft and Teleperformance report that initial client programs piloting the program have seen a 25 percent reduction in call-handling time, a 20 percent reduction in email response times, increased customer satisfaction scores, 90 percent improvement in accurately addressing customer needs, as well as a 35 percent increase in sales conversions and near real-time insights on customer interactions.

All aspects of customer experience will be forever affected by customer service with AI. But we're still in the nascent phase. Customer service is set to be very disrupted by artificial intelligence.[13] Consider the words of Nvidia CEO Jensen Huang who said in November 2023 at the New York Times' DealBook Summit that artificial intelligence will be "fairly competitive" with humans in as few as five years. AI is a set of algorithms, or models, that are trained with massive amounts of data. The algorithms provide recommendations in real time. This can include automation to making recommendations to a human to prompting a specific action. AI leverages massive amounts of data to predict what will happen in the future. The more data you feed the AI, the smarter and more accurate it gets. For example, Walmart has the world's largest data set in the world. After all, they are the biggest company in the world. Walmart is doubling down on technology and AI. In 2022 alone, Walmart invested $14 billion in automation, technology, supply chain, and customer-facing initiatives. Walmart underwent a digital transformation and updated its store layouts to be more customer friendly with a touchless payment app. Walmart's AI strategy is to figure out what the customer wants and provide it in real time. Customers are generating breadcrumbs about what they like and want. Walmart looks at the overall end-to-end picture to enable improvements throughout the entire shopping journey and across the organization, from supply chain management and shopping to search. Sam's Club, owned by Walmart, has floor scrubbers equipped with inventory intelligence towers that take more than twenty million photos of everything on Sam's Club shelves every day. Walmart is testing shelf-scanning robots in dozens of its stores. They are using AI for inventory accuracy to boost its warehouses' capacity to receive and ship products to stores.[14]

Advanced analytics and algorithms can simulate human intelligence in the form of natural language processing, speech recognition, computer vision, and automation. Visual search technology is becoming increasingly popular, as it's faster and more intuitive than traditional keyword searches. Not only does it make shopping easier and more efficient, but it also offers interesting opportunities for personalization, such as giving shoppers the ability to search for items that match their unique style and taste.

Google just announced a new virtual try-on feature that uses generative AI, the same technology underpinning a new crop of chatbots and image creation tools, to show clothes on a wide selection of body types. According to the National Retail Federation, online clothing returns exceed 25 percent, with size and fit being the number one reason for returns. If customers can order more accurately, there will be fewer returns, which means less financial loss for companies, and the environmental benefits of fewer packages on the road. With the visual matching algorithm from Google, shoppers can see how an item would drape, fold, cling, stretch, or form wrinkles and shadows on a diverse set of models in various poses, according to the company.[15] The feature will initially work with women's tops from brands such as Anthropology, Loft, H&M, and Everlane.

Every retailer today wants to differentiate by unlocking unique customer experiences, and they are using technology to do that. AI is already changing the way we shop now. There are a few use cases that are already showing promising results. For example, Estée Lauder and UK retailer Superdrug offer personalized AI- and AR-powered experiences for makeup, skin care, hair care, and wellness. One of the features includes personalized product recommendations and advertising copy.[16] With the use of AI-powered personalization, Superdrug saw a 29 percent rise in average order value, a 70 percent uplift in conversions, and higher customer engagement. They found that with their personalization strategy a customer is two to three times more likely to become a repeat customer.

American grocer Kroger has launched an app that customizes product recommendations with their smart shelves.[17] When a customer walks down an aisle and has their Kroger app open, sensors identify the shopper and highlight products they might be interested in.

Wendy's is the first fast-food chain to offer an AI-powered drive-through. Their new AI chatbot takes orders from customers. The automated ordering experience can engage in conversations with customers, understand made-to-order requests, and generate responses to frequently asked questions.[18] More than 75 percent of Wendy's traffic comes from the drive-through. Their goal is to improve speed, accuracy, and efficiency. I assume they also aim to cut labor costs. By 2025, 95 percent of all customer interactions are predicted to be powered by AI, and it will be because of the convenience and effortlessness such services provide.[19]

Fast food is one area already all in on AI, and it's not just Wendy's. Chatbots are taking orders at White Castle, McDonald's, and Dunkin' drive-throughs, the *Wall Street Journal* reports, and the experience is getting mixed reviews.[20]

Right now the technology is moving faster than the general population's understanding of it and the government's regulation of it. It used to be the reverse. In the 1980s we got our best innovations from the government, like in 1983 when Ronald Reagan approved civilian use of the Pentagon's Global Positioning System, also known as GPS. Now the opposite is true, and the technology/civilian business world is giving the government the best technologies, and the government is slow to figure out what the implications of those technologies are. There is little regulation now other than GDPR, the European privacy rules. *TechCrunch* reported concern about ChatGPT-maker OpenAI's ability to comply with GDPR after a detailed complaint was filed with the Polish data protection authority. The complaint alleged OpenAI is in breach "across a sweep of dimensions: Lawful basis, transparency, fairness, data access rights, and privacy by design."[21]

In the digital world of customer experience, business leaders are already tasked with ethical conundrums. Just because we can, does that mean we should? These ethical questions are not just about AI; they are about customer data, customer privacy, and how far companies should go to win. Business and technology leaders have to be the voice of ethics for a government that simply can't move quickly enough to protect society.

A consultant shared with me the story of a bank that would target customers paying off mortgages using their debit accounts: the bank could target those customers to switch their mortgage to this bank. The same bank wanted to force employees to bank with them, the employer, so the paycheck could only be deposited in the employer's bank accounts. Bank executives were concerned that their money was going to competitors. Employees were concerned with the confidentiality of their earned wages. While the bank never succeeded in forcing employees to deposit money in their employer's accounts, it's still concerning. One wonders what the executives of that bank were thinking. Did the bank purely have a culture of greed? Or was the pressure on these executives so extreme they were willing to be unethical in order to meet their performance metrics? Or both? Is it better to set the bar so high you can't achieve the goal so you risk your teams acting unethical to meet those impossible standards? No, of course it's not better. What is better is to be real about what's reasonable and possible for the business and achieve goals that are in the grasp of the employee without doing something unethical.

This story is a reminder that just because you *can* doesn't mean you *should*. Should all customer-facing agents be replaced with AI? That would be a disaster. There are many questions leaders must be asking themselves, including the following:

- "What do I stand for, as a leader?" Not simply "What can the technology do?"

- "Do I want the technology to do that?"

- "Would I offer the experience I'm delivering to customers to my parents, my spouse, or my kids?"

You must create a company that's ethical, that you feel proud of. And from there, what do you stand for as a team, and as a company? You are currently creating a world for your children and grandchildren—no matter your age or if you even have children. Just because a business can make money today on a technology that should not be unleashed on the world doesn't mean you should. Today, being a leader is being a chess player. Every action has a reaction. Every company should not just be doing journey mapping for customers but also for the future. How is your company going to continue to transform, and as the company transforms with the exponential growth of technology, what ethics and standards should be your guiding light?

Ethics and standards matter a great deal; they matter as much as the product categories you enter. A business can start making a lot of money, but if the leadership isn't strong, and the foresight isn't there, it's likely there will be a bubble that bursts.

STORYTELLING WITH STYLE: TY INC.

Ty Warner founded Ty Inc. in 1986 and released Beanie Babies in 1993, which became a global sensation. He under-stuffed the toys to make them more huggable by filling them with plastic beads instead of cloth stuffing and made them small enough to fit anywhere. Beanie Babies animals each come with tiny poems on their tags.[22] The Beanie Baby craze, which inspired a collecting frenzy, was powered in part by a 1999 *People* magazine article and a group of Illinois moms who helped fuel a thriving black market for the toys and drove prices even higher.[23]

By the mid-1990s, Beanie Babies became wildly popular, with special edition toys made in partnership with businesses like McDonald's and Wrigley Field. Beanie Babies became extremely valuable, with particular styles worth thousands of dollars, thanks to the internet and eBay. Ty Inc. built the world's first business-to-consumer website. Customers started collecting Beanie Babies like they were baseball cards. Ty Inc. became one of the world's most profitable toy companies, hitting more than $1 billion per year in sales at its height. Unfortunately the CEO was not a futurist and was not a good leader or manager. His reputation is spotty. In 2014, he was prosecuted and convicted for tax evasion,[24] and more recently ugly charges have been thrown against him from personal relationships. Stories of his unorthodox management style have surfaced.

Ty Inc. slowly ran itself into the ground thanks to bad management and lack of foresight. This was all captured in a recent film on Apple TV called *The Beanie Baby Bubble*. Ty Warner is presented as an eccentric, unprofessional, and immature adult that mixes personal and professional relationships. Leadership is not to be treated lightly—heavy is the head that wears the crown, and you better understand that every single thing you do will be reviewed with a microscope. So, not only do you need to have a unique product, but all aspects around taking that product to market are incredibly important, and leadership and culture are absolutely critical. No amount of innovation and new technology can change that.

With all that said, many Beanie Babies are still valuable. Today if you can pair a group of Beanie Babies together like the Large Wallace Ty (a green teddy with a red check scarf) with two regular-sized Wallaces and his bear pals Cashew and Huggy, you will get a 600K reward for them.[25] Bubbles, a small yellow and black fish, with a poem about him, is worth as much as $129,000 today. But the mismanagement of the company ran the business into the ground by overproducing the product, and the Beanie Baby bubble burst.

Ty Inc. benefited from the technology innovation of how customers buy, and the innovation happening at the time of the product creation was more important than the idea for the product. eBay made Ty Inc. a billion-dollar company.

Did anyone in the '80s predict small stuffed animals made with a different stuffing would skyrocket in value to thousands of dollars? No, but with improvements in the internet and computers you could have predicted the computer would make its way into the customer's shopping habits. But being a fad run by an unpredictable and emotional leader is a dangerous position to be in. Ty Inc.'s success was an accident. It wasn't a result of customer-focused leadership; they were lucky that Beanie Babies became a collector's item for a time.

The best position to be in is to build a role in the customer's life based on delivering value no one else is delivering. Whatever is going on "out there," you must create a relationship based on trust so that even if other brands offer the same product or service, the customer trusts that you will always deliver on your customer promise.

Ty Inc. reminds us that the marketing of the product can be almost as important as the product itself. Ty Inc. greatly profited from the invention of eBay, which catapulted Beanie Babies. The experience around the product can catapult a product that has copycats above the rest. But no matter how innovative the product or delivery, bad management and leadership will ultimately bring its demise.

DEALING WITH UNCERTAINTY
AND PIVOTING ON A DIME

In business and in life, often things do not go as planned. Dealing with uncertainty is not always bad, but a disruption in regularly scheduled programming can be interruptive. I've thought about this quite a bit in my own life. I have little kids, a mortgage, aging dogs—there's always something that generally needs attention that I had not factored into my day. Most of you reading this probably have your own interruptive incidents that spring out of left field. But if you accept the unforeseen circumstance, it's much easier. I think about this as the Pareto principle, also known as the 80/20 rule. Eighty percent of life and work is predictable—things run as usual, everything going to plan. But 20 percent of the time things come out of left field. Family members get sick, cars break down, plans don't work out as imagined. So you are perpetually dealing with 20 percent of uncertainty and stressful incidents. As you get older and have kids, this goes up. Accepting that 20 percent of your plans are always going to get rerouted will make you a better leader, family member, and person. It's like an experiment with which you cannot control all variables, so accepting that part of the experiment will not go as planned is critical.

How does the 80/20 rule relate to leadership? As a leader, one-fifth of your work is going to be in flux. That should inspire you to take more risks, because even with the risks you do not take, there can still be variation. Therefore you're better off being bold and trying new strategies, knowing nothing in life is certain, even the tools you've depended on for years.

STORYTELLING WITH STYLE: BED
BATH & BEYOND GOES BUST

There are many headlines about the "end of retail," but I believe this is actually *the beginning of retail*, albeit a better retail that's more personalized and customer centric. You probably have a Bed Bath & Beyond 20 percent off coupon floating around somewhere in your junk drawer. Here's a store that was larger than life in the early 2000s. It was once an unstoppable retailer, called a "category killer" for its triumph over many rivals.[26] But as time went on, Bed Bath & Beyond lost its relevance. Bed Bath & Beyond, according to many, simply missed the boat on the internet. They were trying to be too many things to too many people. They had no identity and lost their place in the customer's life. Bed Bath & Beyond has experienced a turbulent few years, and after several misfired turnarounds, abrupt leadership shake-ups, stock issues, store closures, job cuts, and numerous last-gasp financing deals, the company is going bankrupt. For months, the chain has been losing both money and shoppers, struggling to restock shelves as suppliers and banks cut off its credit. This is an example of how you are never too big to fail.

The year 2020 expedited the death of many retail stores with more than twelve thousand closing. Bed Bath & Beyond plans to begin closing its 360 stores and 120 Buy Buy Baby stores.

David's Bridal is another story of a behemoth of a retailer that could not fix its issues fast enough. The turnaround CEO Jim Marcum, who arrived on the scene in 2020, walked into the headquarters in Pittsburgh to make the company customer centric. He fired all the consultants, brought his top executives into a room with a whiteboard, rolled up his sleeves, and told the team they were about to start working a lot differently. He asked everyone to start waking up at 6:00 a.m. to understand where the company had gone wrong with customers by reading poor reviews of the stores online.

Marcum instituted a digital transformation creating a more seamless shopping experience for a customer that was now using their devices to shop and plan for their wedding. They instituted a customer loyalty program and renewed the company's commitment to the customer. And even during and after COVID, things were looking up. After emerging from bankruptcy in 2019, the new CEO said, "David's Bridal represents a phenomenal opportunity. It's 25 percent of the bridal industry today." Their Net Promoter Score went from forty to eighty. The culture was starting to improve.[27]

But it was too little, too late, and in 2023 the company again filed for bankruptcy. The company could not make up for lost time, and they had been asleep for too long. If you are unable to be customer centric and you are missing the boat on the who, what, where, why, and how of the customer experience, your fate is uncertain. No one is too big to fail.

THERE ARE MANY challenges for operating retail stores today, not just the disruption from the internet. The year 2023 wasn't a great year for retailers, either, because of "shrink." Shrink is the loss of inventory that can be attributed to factors such as employee theft, shoplifting, administrative error, vendor fraud, damage, and cashier error. Increasingly this category has been affected by rising crime, especially in urban centers.[28]

At Lowe's alone in 2023, shrink cost them $1 billion.[29] Target predicted a $1.3 billion loss from shrink in 2023.[30] CEO Brian Cornell said, "We are making significant investments in strategies to prevent this from happening in our stores and protect our guests and our team. We're also focused on managing the financial impact on our business so we can continue to keep our stores open, knowing they create local jobs and offer convenient access to essentials."

But it's a challenge across the country, particularly in California. A 2022 California crime report revealed that the state's violent crime rate increased by 6.1 percent since 2021, and property crime was up 6.2 percent.[31]

My friend was with her kids at Nordstrom Topanga in Woodland Hills, California, when a flash mob sprayed the security guard with bear pepper spray. They stole $100,000 of merchandise. My friend hid in the dressing room with her two little kids trying to keep them calm as chaos erupted on the first floor. This is a frequent news headline in California, and one wonders why retailers still have stores at all when they are being robbed frequently and casually. Employees feel unsafe and customers stick to online orders, which are less risky. Companies must think about the realities of society today and how they can move forward while being honest about what is happening outside their business's doors. Technology can be a great help to keep retailers safe, but the question also lingers: How much will in-store retail stay the same?

THE CHANGING FACE OF RETAIL

Half of US Gen Z social users make purchases on social media, according to data from Insider Intelligence.[32] As many as 57 percent of Gen Z shoppers—or close to three in five—say they get items like clothing and shoes over the internet.[33] This is followed by groceries, 24 percent; automobile parts or accessories, 21 percent; pharmaceutical products, 21 percent; home and garden, 21 percent; and children's products, 19 percent.

Gen Z is the generation most likely to use buy now, pay later services to make a purchase, and they are also embracing other emerging digital payment technologies like mobile wallets, contactless solutions, and peer-to-peer payment apps.

STORYTELLING WITH STYLE:
DOMINO'S

We can remember back in 2012 when the then Domino's CEO proclaimed that every company "is a technology company." The company invested millions of dollars over the next few years on transforming Domino's into the largest pizza company in the world with 15,900 stores in eighty-five countries and almost $18 billion in annual revenue. The next biggest pizza chain is Pizza Hut with $13 billion in revenue per year. In 2018, *Forbes* contributor Brian Solis interviewed their chief digital officer, Dennis Malone, who said about their success at making the pizza company more like an e-commerce company: "Our marketing and IT groups actually work together. Everyone on both of those teams is trying to achieve the same goals. We win together, we fail together."[34] There are more than fifteen ways to order pizza ranging from sending a pizza emoji over social media to a voice command on Google Home.

Increasingly, executives are having to learn more about technologies they never had to think about before. But you cannot just throw technology at a situation and expect the situation to fix itself. In fact, if employees do not like the technology, they won't use it.

Jeff Bezos once said that it is just as important to pay attention to what customer trends don't change, like customer demand around low prices, vast selection, and fast delivery.[35] It's as important to pay attention to customer preferences that remain constant as it is to pay attention to what *does* change. Most companies don't need as much futurism as they just need to understand that in the future customer experience demands are only increasing, not decreasing. Many are not even meeting the table stakes of customer experience.

STORYTELLING WITH STYLE:
DAVID GEFFEN

David Geffen is an innovator and one of the most prolific content creators and enablers of the twentieth century whom you've likely never heard of. David was born in Brooklyn, New York, to Ukrainian immigrants with no money to their name. His mother had a sewing and tailor shop. David was not a good student and never went to college, but he finagled a job at the William Morris agency in the mail room by lying on his résumé. But David knew if they found out he lied he would surely be canned. He heard a rumor that a trainee was fired for lying on their application. David couldn't let that happen. He came in early for four months to intercept the disastrous letter from UCLA saying that Geffen never went to school there. When the letter came, Geffen had UCLA stationary printed, forged a new letter, and had someone he knew remail it from LA confirming his attendance.

Geffen was always resourceful, resilient, and scrappy. He was someone who had the vision to become one of the first successful music agents in history. He negotiated good deals for his musicians at Asylum Records, a generator of the Southern California folk-rock sound. He signed artists such as the Eagles, Joni Mitchell, Bob Dylan, Tom Waits, Aerosmith, and Guns N' Roses. Geffen's own fear that his life would not be meaningful motivated him to be an incredibly successful entrepreneurial businessperson. It's Geffen's vision that has left him with a reputation in the industry as a futurist. He saw opportunities others did not see. David Geffen created the major music sounds of the '60s, '70s, '80s, and even '90s. Asylum Records was sold in 1993 for a few million dollars in cash and $10 million in Warner stock. In 1980, David Geffen formed his second record company, called Geffen Records. The company eventually struggled, and his investors and partners lost faith in the company. Geffen Records was not creating hits, and David knew he needed a completely new strategy. He had the opportunity to get out of the business, but instead he surrounded himself with music scouts who had their ear to the ground on what customers would like. He did not intend to lose.

These scouts discovered and developed bands like Guns N' Roses for years with hits like "Welcome to the Jungle" and "Sweet Child O' Mine" as well as Nirvana's "Smells Like Teen Spirit" and "Come as You Are." These sounds often took years to build. Geffen Records turned out hit after hit, shaping the major sounds of the '80s and '90s. He took a company that had almost zero value to selling the company to MCA Inc. for more than $550 million in stock in less than ten years, making Geffen one of America's richest people at the time.

He then started his third company, a movie studio called Dream-Works with Steven Spielberg and Jeffrey Katzenberg. No one had created a new movie studio in fifty years, and it was a huge risk at the time. It was a unique partnership, and together these business-men created groundbreaking content—films like *Almost Famous*, *Castaway*, and *Gladiator*. In 2006, DreamWorks sold to Viacom for $100 million. Geffen created three companies on his own by taking huge risks, and these risks have paid off, making him the wealthiest person in the entertainment industry at $11 billion.[36]

So what do customer experience leaders have to learn from David Geffen? At every step, David was making moves based on gut and intuition, not an assurance that his efforts would gener-ate a return. David was not born a futurist, but he had very solid intuition, and most of all he knew to surround himself with people that knew where the culture was headed and saw trends starting to take shape.

David was a visionary and had no problem ignoring the metrics that he knew weren't a measure of the potential for his businesses. There is an art to business; it builds relationships and engenders loyalty and fandom. But how can you measure art by looking at metrics used to measure what worked in the past?

If you ran your customer strategy like David Geffen, how would it be different? Perhaps you would take more risks and understand the value of building relationships, taking risks on new pursuits you might not have thought of. The question you must always ask is, if you could no longer sell the products you sell now, what would you sell? You would likely allow agents to go outside of their scope if it meant a better outcome. You might take a risk on a new technology or process, without knowing if it's 100 percent fool-proof. You would not just predict the future—you would create it.

Some leaders are bold futurists, moving too fast for the world, even alienating and offending some. While others are way too insular, not bringing in outside counsel to tell them when they have their head in the sand. The ideal customer-centric leader that is also a futurist is able to ride in the middle. The fact is customer experience cannot save your company from being disrupted. If your leadership is stale and your model is outdated, problems will arise.

For customer experience leaders, the cone of possibilities framework on the next page provides a structured way to think about the future of customer experience, anticipate various scenarios, and plan accordingly. There are a few ways you can think about the sections of the cone. The common way that is taught is as follows (see also figure 7-1):

Probable Future. The central part of the cone represents the most likely outcomes based on current trends and data. Examples could be increased use of AI in the contact center, the demise of retail stores and transformation into experience centers, the continued consumerization of health care, and so on.

Plausible Future. As we move outward, these scenarios are possible but less certain. They're based on potential shifts in current trends.

The Cone of Possibilities

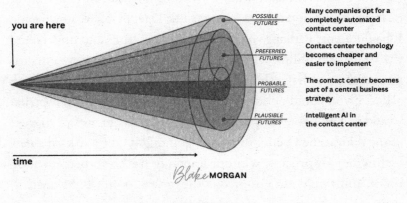

FIGURE 7-1

Examples for customer experience would be more attention paid to the contact center by senior leadership and the CMO, the rise of new channels such as video chat, and increased personalization from brands as customer expectations, particularly from Gen Z, increase. Companies become much more aware of their environmental impact as customers become increasingly aware of the damage the lack of corporate oversight has done to the environment, and companies all over the world start making major changes to create a more sustainable future.

Possible Future. Further out, these scenarios might seem unlikely right now but could occur if certain conditions change. Examples of this could be, first, the idea that your entire customer experience will be automated and customers won't want to interact with a person. Or second, the idea that biometrics will replace IDs and passports in airports and other places. Or third, in the next ten to fifteen years, the world will move to fully self-driving vehicles.

Preposterous Future. The outer edges of the cone represent wild, speculative scenarios. While they seem far-fetched, they challenge our assumptions and spark creativity. The preposterous future examples might include a contact center without a person in it, fully emotionally intelligent robots handling all customer issues, and the complete disappearance of jobs for humans.

A structure we can use to think through scenarios can be as follows:

1. Imagine various scenarios.

2. Collect information and insights.

3. Horizon Scan (triggers/indicators).

4. Create an action plan.

Let's look at an example for each.

1. Probable future: The demise of retail stores, and continued rapid and aggressive growth of digital.

Information and insights: In-store retail has taken a hit. Not only are many transactions moving online, but having a retail store at all creates a liability with theft and crime on the rise. Customers are enjoying an increasingly seamless, zero friction experience from online shopping, and more brands are making it easy with augmented reality to experience an item virtually and free returns if it doesn't work out.

Horizon Scan: So many direct-to-consumer brands are exploding in popularity, showing today that you don't need the headache and overhead that a retail store provides. It's no secret the emerging direct-to-consumer business model has disrupted and transformed the e-commerce industry. A growing number of companies design, manufacture, market, sell, and ship their products themselves, without intermediaries. In 2022, approximately 64 percent of consumers worldwide made regular purchases directly from brands.

It's estimated the total number of purchases in 2023 was $182 billion. The market size is forecast to grow to almost $213 billion by 2024.[37]

Action plan: Consider if you actually need to run your retail presence as you did in the past.

How can you create a beautiful and seamless customer experience directly to the consumer with digital and cut costs by owning more of the production process of your company?

Experience other brands that offer compelling direct-to-consumer experiences from a variety of industries such as retail (Warby Parker, Casper, or Away Luggage) and imagine what it would be like for your brand to be inspired by what they offer.

2. Plausible future:

Information and insights: It's plausible that the contact center will become a hotbed of innovation and will secure much more respect, funding, and attention. More employees will want to work in the contact center and find roles with the word *customer* in them. More attention will be paid to the contact center by senior leadership. As the operational costs of running a contact center go down, companies will be able to better compete on experience, including adding value to customers' lives in new and compelling ways.

Horizon Scan: Today, 95 percent of customers say customer service has an impact on brand loyalty.[38] This is the direction the world is headed. With so much research showing how customer-focused companies are more profitable—and the correlation between good experience and higher profits—it becomes much easier for customer experience leaders to secure funding for their programs. Increasingly, good companies are competing on experience.

Action plan: Do an audit of your current customer experience offered by your company.

Create your own analysis, based on the customer feedback, of where your company is and where it needs to be.

Meet with the various business unit heads to discuss and make the business case to your CEO or board.

Create a plan to secure funding for these programs and show how you will save or make the company money.

3. Possible future: Your entire customer experience will be automated, and customers won't want to interact with a person.

Information and insights: Many customer experiences today have all but removed people. Some companies (many of them are software companies) like Moz, Wistia, and Squarespace do not have people that work in the contact center anymore at all. And as we mentioned earlier in the book, Frontier Airlines also cut the call center. It is one possible scenario that the contact centers of the future won't actually have people working in them.

Horizon Scan: Breakthroughs in machine learning and AI are able to listen to the customer and provide a correct solution to their problem. The worldwide adoption of robotics is expected to reach $107.3 billion in 2025, up from $7.6 billion in 2018, says the report "Artificial Intelligence Market Forecasts," based on research from Tractica.[39] In the future it's possible improved emotionally intelligent AI could replace a human contact center agent. But do customers like this? In a 2022 survey about chatbots, about 50 percent said they were comfortable using it to ask about a product, but only 23 percent of the respondents said they would trust a chatbot to settle disputes, and only about a third would trust the chatbot to pay a bill.[40] More than half (54 percent) were uncomfortable if the chatbot tried to impersonate a human. But as the technology improves, it is likely the AI could make experiences more efficient, allowing contact center agents to spend more time advising customers or even proactively reaching out to them to add value to their lives in other ways.

Action plan: Survey your customers to ask them about how they feel regarding AI. Understand where you would be able to use it to add value to the employee and customer experience, and where it might be unwelcome.

Ensure your employees are educated on advances in machine learning and AI and understand what other industries are doing.

Engage with regulatory bodies to understand where privacy, data laws, and AI collide.

Figure out if your contact center did have more automation, how you would continue to invest in creating a human experience in the contact center.

4. Preposterous future: Thanks to advances in AI, you can literally run a company with no people in it. The robots will be calling the shots.

Information and insights: With so much discussion of AI taking over for human beings, is it that preposterous to think that we will be facing a future world where there simply are no humans making any decisions at all?

Horizon Scan: AI could make autonomous decisions if we allowed it to. Remember the film *Her* from 2013? That is possible today. We can program an AI to think like a person, and advances in AI in the last year have even furthered this reality. Examples include: (1) Space probes that travel vast distances and carry out tasks in space without real-time human control; (2) Grocery-bagging droids that can package grocery items autonomously; (3) Kamikaze drones designed for specific missions; and (4) "Joggobot," a flying device that operates autonomously and flies beside a person while they are running.[41]

Action plan: Ensure those who are making technology decisions for your company are extremely thoughtful, ethical, and measured people.

Think about the further-down-the-line implications of what you are doing.

Ask yourself what kind of society you want for your children, and don't just think of them; think of future generations and the future of life on Earth.

EXERCISE

This is a high-level framework that you can use for strategic business decisions, planning, and even general critical thinking exercises.

Ask employees to write in a curiosity journal where they can just brainstorm, ask questions, or pinpoint specific customer experience trends they are paying attention to.

Host a monthly customer experience "what if" session where employees can come together and share ideas around specific prompts.

Create diverse teams where employees have different perspectives, points of views, and skills. This will ensure that whenever you are brainstorming potential futures that you will get varying ideas.

Experiment with backcasting. This involves you imagining it's a future date (say, 2035) and that you have hit all of your goals and projections. Work backward from there to imagine what you had to do to get there and the milestones you had to hit along the way.

Foresight is about being proactive and not just reactive. It's about trying to identify the future customer experience you would want for yourself and then taking steps to create that future. Leaders who embed foresight into their strategy not only navigate the future with confidence but also shape it.

In an era marked by uncertainty and volatility, the ability to think ahead, anticipate change, and act proactively is what differentiates successful leaders from the rest.

8

---

*Law 6: Don't Forget
That Employees Are Customers Too*

When Doc Rivers took over as the head basketball coach of the Boston Celtics, he wasn't sure how he was going to lead the team to victory. A longtime board member at Marquette University, Rivers was leaving a meeting one day when a colleague came up to him. "Your team is going to be amazing . . . have you ever heard of 'Ubuntu'?" She urged him to look up the concept, telling him, "It's not a word, Doc. It's a way of life." He stayed up all night studying Ubuntu, an African proverb that means "I am because we are" or "I can't be all I can be unless you can be all you can be." The phrase, which Rivers learned more about from Archbishop Desmond Tutu and Nelson Mandela, reminds players, fellow coaches, and everyone involved that they can achieve what they want to only by making those around them better.

Doc took over the head coaching role for the Celtics in 2004. The Celtics had not won one a championship since 1986. Doc's aha leadership moment did not come about until three years later. The Celtics had acquired three superstar players, Ray Allen, Kevin Garnett, and Paul Pierce, in a pair of blockbuster trades, making themselves into overnight championship contenders. The members of this trio each boasted numerous individual accolades, but none had ever made it to the NBA Finals. Doc was afraid that they would compete to be individually successful but not work well together as a team.

In order to keep his team focused on team success instead of individual glory, Rivers instilled the principle of Ubuntu during the team's 2007 training camp in Italy, and it became the battle cry of the Celtics as they embarked on their run to the 2008 championship. The team worked together beautifully, passing the ball, with no one player trying to outshine everyone else. By stressing from the outset the importance of sharing the ball and trusting teammates, Rivers was able to get his three stars to mesh instantly. All three averaged more than 17 points per game as Boston finished with a 66–16 record, the best in the NBA. The Celtics shocked the world by winning the 2008 championship, all thanks to a little teamwork and a philosophy of "we" over "me."

Leaders today must remember they are not coaching individuals. They are coaching teams. Imagine if Ubuntu was put into place at your company. How would divisions work together better than they do now? Or how would your own teammates drop any drama or politics to collaborate around one goal?

If you have one superstar salesperson, and that creates a competitive culture, that's a problem for your entire team and company. You will have to find a way to create that team environment, just like Doc Rivers did with the Boston Celtics. How willing is your team to pass the ball so the entire team can win, versus individual ego? It is the culture you create that determines whether the team wants to work together or just focus on their own success.

THE BUSINESS WORLD already knew a few years ago that employee engagement had taken a nosedive, but the research today shows that employees still need more support. Employees do not feel engaged in their work; they are not showing up fully for work. In early 2022, US employee engagement slumped to a seven-year low with 32 percent of employees engaged and 17 percent actively disengaged at work. And in 2023, engagement levels in the US dropped two percentage points. That means less than one-third of your employees are engaged.[1] Why does this matter for the customer-focused company?

Every team must have a great coach, and that great coach can be you. If you want to be a customer-focused company, you must start with the type of leader you want to be. A customer-focused culture is a coached culture of employees that genuinely feel part of a team. The culture must reward teamwork over praising individual superstar behavior and pitting individuals against one another.

Creating a customer-focused company is an exercise in leadership, and that leadership is a group of coaches rather than a group of business managers.

Customer experience is not just about creating incredible products, marketing them in an innovative way, and providing the best customer service. It's an entirely new way of thinking. But that entirely new way of thinking requires the mindset of a coach— building and developing a team. That coaching mentality never sleeps. The goal is to create a business that people love, that creates good quality and unique products and experiences. But you do that through the people that make up the team.

A customer-focused company is not just a leader and their customers. The team is the secret sauce that leads to a business that customers can't get enough of. You practice how you play, and the enthusiasm for the drudgery of practice, and paying attention to all the minutiae and details, is what makes the team perform strong when it counts. The facts don't lie—85 percent of respondents to a recent IDC survey agree that an improved employee experience and higher employee engagement translate to a better customer experience, higher customer satisfaction, and higher revenues for their company.[2] Additionally, 62 percent said that employee experience and customer experience have a defined causal relationship and that the impact was "large" or "significant" and measurable. Over half (58 percent) indicated that customer satisfaction is a key metric in evaluating employee productivity. It's the chicken or the egg—a good employee experience drives high customer satisfaction, and customers that are less stressed create happier employees. It works both ways.

As a customer-centric leader-coach, you are engaging your team. You are constantly bringing your team back to the shared vision of your company. You are guiding them toward the North Star, and you do that meeting by meeting, day by day. This is another example of the need for wash, rinse, repeat: coaching is an every-week thing, not a one-and-done situation. Bill Campbell, the former CEO of Intuit and beloved business coach, said this: "Great coaches lie awake at night thinking about how to make you better. They relish creating an environment where you get more out of yourself. Coaches are like great artists getting the stroke exactly right on a painting. They are painting relationships."

It's like being a parent; most parents think about the well-being of their kids 24-7. There is extreme ownership, because "if it's going to be, it's up to me" (well, in this case, you!). When you care about your kids, or your employees, you are in the background preparing the circumstances for their success even when they have no idea you're doing it. You're doing what's best for your employees, your customers, and the business overall, always trying to make win-win-win situations. Technology can help leaders do that.

STORYTELLING WITH STYLE: NATIONWIDE

I recently interviewed Amy Shore, the chief customer officer for Nationwide. She told me about her internal enterprise tool at Nationwide, The Voice, that collects associate feedback to enhance the customer and partner (agent, financial professional) experiences. More than eighty-one hundred associates have access to the tool and have submitted more than 5,450 ideas to improve the customer experience, of which 20–40 percent are actionable and have been implemented or included in larger projects. According to Shore and her team, The Voice aligns business priorities, engages associates (employees), and fosters a customer-centric approach. It provides a direct channel for leaders to recognize associates and prioritize enhancements based on their valuable insights, contributing to positive business results and a more seamless, caring experience for all stakeholders.

Another big improvement came when a group within Nationwide Financial received multiple submissions through The Voice regarding its less-than-efficient bank account verification process. Many local banks and credit unions do not proactively supply bank account information to the vendor Nationwide uses to verify this information, which resulted in numerous follow-up calls. To improve this process, this business area implemented steps to verbally "preverify" the bank account holder's name(s) and account numbers up front when a customer or financial professional calls to get a withdrawal form and when they want an automatic deposit. When placing outbound calls, associates used to need members to fulfill privacy requirements before they could discuss their account. This created confusion for members who were concerned for their security during a call they did not initiate. An associate engaged through The Voice recommended a more effortless flow that they used via email. Your customer-facing employees have their finger on the pulse of what's happening with customers. Asking contact center agents what is broken with the customer experience, how to create internal efficiencies, and how to reduce back-end complexity is very important.

Every day is game day for today's customer. How you practice is how you play. Every tiny part of how the company is run has cumulative impacts on the customer experience delivered. If you knew every day was game day, wouldn't that affect how you treat your employees? If you are not willing to invest and grow the people that you hire, then you are hiring the wrong people. Every employee should be a teammate that is onboarded, trained, engaged, and developed. The customer experience mindset is caring about your employees, but it's more than that. It's being a coach and running your company like a team. The more you care about customer experience, the more critical it is to spend time with your employees and to think of yourself more as a coach than a manager.

I recently spoke with Brian Dunphy, the former VP of customer experience at Warby Parker, and he told me that he never delivered negative feedback in his office because he didn't want people to feel like they were "going to the principal's office." He would always have hard conversations over lunch, or even at the contact center agent's desk, so the agent would feel more comfortable, in their own space, and more open to hearing feedback. The contact center has some of the worst churn of any industry, ever. But it is the most important place in your entire business: these are the lucky individuals who get to talk to your customers every single day.

Brian Dunphy has seven tactics he uses to engage his employees in the contact center. He's used these tactics at all the places he has worked including Disney, Postmates, Warby Parker, and Asurion. These tactics include (see also figure 8-1):

Engagement Ideas for Contact Center Agents

FIGURE 8-1

1. **Director for the Day.** Brian would swap positions with his agents so his agents would become the director and Brian would take the contact center calls. The agent would participate in senior meetings and have the opportunity to shadow the managers. This also includes becoming familiar with the contact center manager reports and gaining experience around the inner workings of the contact center.

2. **Getting recognition** on giant TV boards throughout the office. This recognition would be for anniversaries, birthdays, or an amazing call an agent had with a customer. This board would also feature comments from customers, including praise for agents. Another way to do this is digitally, with recognition on the intranet celebrating successes, anniversaries, and birthdays.

3. **Handwritten cards from leadership.** Brian would set a reminder to write cards to staff every week, including words of praise and gratitude. He said that eventually every agent was proudly displaying a card on their desk. It was a small act of recognition that agents felt very proud of and would show their family.

4. **Handing out special badge lanyards.** Brian would provide special lanyards to staff to differentiate veteran staff from new hires, with varying colors or beautiful designs. These are small acts that go a long way.

5. **Team lunches.** Brian's team would host lunches for top performers. Lunch-and-learns would be moderated with senior staff, or they'd just enjoy some casual chitchat together. The best part was VPs and directors would serve lunch to the agents, and the agents could relax and enjoy being fussed over.

6. **Remote agents having food delivered**. Remote agents would receive a complimentary lunch while they were being onboarded and gifts for the very "serious" remote agent dress code like a bathrobe, fun-branded pajamas, or sandals.

7. **Agents coach other agents.** Brian felt that a message delivered by peers resonated more than a message delivered by management. One powerful tool would simply be to have agents coach one another. A very high-performing agent could come in and coach a new hire class. And the wisdom coming from a peer would be very effective, more than from a supervisor.

THE CONTACT CENTER is the treasure chest of the company; it's a missed opportunity that most companies never fully appreciate. Smart management of the contact center doesn't have to be expensive. It's just about taking the time to create a culture of kindness and recognition—a little goes a long way.

The path to a customer-focused culture is teamwork and the constant and rigorous attention to what goes on with the people who represent your company. It's a commitment to winning based on collaboration around what is best for the employee, the business, and the customer. When you have the customer experience mindset, then you are always making strategies that are customer centric but also employee centric. You create a culture of accountability, but also of caring.

You can't fake the customer experience mindset. You've got to be out there every day with your teams on the front lines. You have got to flip burgers next to employees, like Lynsi Snyder of In-N-Out Burger.

STORYTELLING WITH STYLE: FLIPPING BURGERS NEXT TO EMPLOYEES AT IN-N-OUT

In-N-Out Burger was started by Harry and Esther Snyder in 1948, when a burger cost twenty-five cents. Harry believed in his ability to create his own opportunities, and Esther believed in Harry. Harry hated cheap food and wanted to use only fresh ingredients. In-N-Out burgers are delicious and that's thanks to the fresh ingredients. If you don't eat In-N-Out yourself, you've probably heard your friends and family talk about Animal Style Fries, one of the most popular items on In-N-Out Burger's "secret menu." These are French fries with cheese, In-N-Out's special spread, and grilled onions right on top. The In-N-Out burger is simple, iconic, and very Americana.

The current president and owner of In-N-Out, Lynsi Snyder— Harry and Esther's granddaughter—landed at the helm of the ship after multiple tragedies. Both of the founders and their sons died early deaths.

Lynsi's uncle Rich Snyder took over the company in 1976 when he was twenty-four years old after his own father died. Then the unthinkable happened: Rich also died when his plane crashed after seeing his niece Lynsi in a play. Lynsi's father, Guy Snyder, took over the company in 1993. But things went from bad to worse when her father experienced congestive heart failure as a result of opioid use in 1999.

Lynsi had worked at In-N-Out for years in various roles: leafing lettuce when she was seventeen, alternating between backroom and cashier work. During her first marriage, she moved to In-N-Out Burger's headquarters in Baldwin Park, California, to take a job working for her grandmother in donations for the charity foundation. Then she managed the merchandising department for more than two years. In the next few years, she familiarized herself with the operations rotating different jobs and was trained by her grandmother Esther. Lynsi became president and CEO in 2010 when she was just twenty-eight years old.

In the years before this, when she was between twenty and twenty-two years old, she partied and partook in alcohol and marijuana. She said of that time, "It was like a black-sheep era of my life." Although married four times, she doesn't hide what she went through. She took all the pain of her past and used it as fuel to become a very empathic leader. Today she is a top-rated president, beloved by her employees. Snyder has gained a lot of recognition on Glassdoor for being so beloved by her employees with a 96 percent approval rating. She leads by example because she is a self-described "servant leader," and her employees agree.

Lynsi wants to lead from the back and discussed it in an interview about Glassdoor's Employer of Choice awards: "I prefer that our leaders [at In-N-Out] adopt a servant leadership style, and I try to lead by example. It's hard to argue with the approach that puts your people and their well-being first. The shortest road to connected *associates* is to lead them as they would like to be led."

The story of the Snyder family is a story of tragedy, heartbreak, and triumph. And at the heart of the story is now a very powerful president who has proved the skeptics wrong.

Lynsi has continued to preserve the legacy, and she uses the customer experience mindset to do so. She said, "One of the values that has changed my world is humility. Growing up, there was a time where I thought I needed to hide my father's drug addiction . . . but I've found so much freedom in being honest and open with those things. People are going to judge you; let them judge you but based on the truth." One of the tenets of the customer experience mindset is authenticity. When you aren't destroyed by your demons, and you aren't ashamed of your past, you become the hero of your own story. When you figure out how to show up in the world, leading from a place of strength, others have something to learn from you.

> *You are who you are. A lion doesn't walk into the Sahara and say, "I'm a lion." All the animals already know it's a lion.*
> —LYNSI SNYDER, CEO, IN-N-OUT

Snyder doesn't look like a president billionaire businesswoman at first glance. She has tattoos and wears clothes that I wouldn't describe as business casual. She doesn't care much about what others think. She and her family have been through enough to know what matters—sticking to what works and not wavering. Snyder said, "It's not about the money for us. . . . Unless God sends a lightning bolt down and changes my heart miraculously, I would not ever sell [In-N-Out]." Snyder is fiercely protective of her family's legacy, and In-N-Out is not for sale. Snyder has stuck to the tenets of the employee experience while also sticking to the uniformity and staples of the business that made it so successful. And customers are extremely loyal to the brand.

Lynsi Snyder is consumed with providing value to the customer and knowing what the customer likes. The company's decisions are led by protecting her family's legacy and doing what is better for the customer, not what will make more profit for the company in the short term. Staying true to the tenets of what make In-N-Out great is what makes Lynsi a customer experience futurist: she knows that customers don't need a new type of burger every month but love the original recipes.

Snyder has grown the company from 295 locations in 2017 to more than 400 locations today.[3]

Not much has changed about In-N-Out since 1948, including the ingredients. The price is lower than competitors, even as their employee wages increase. You will not find a new bacon-wrapped idea on the menu. Their buns are baked with slow-rising sponge dough, and each morning all the fresh meat (never frozen) is ground by three facilities, delivering daily to restaurants. In-N-Out does not franchise. Heat lamps, microwaves, and freezers are banned from the premises. The recipes for its burgers and fries have remained the same for seventy-five years.

In-N-Out is one of the rare brands that is both lowbrow and highbrow—it was a favorite at *Vanity Fair* Oscar parties[4] and was the favorite LA hot spot of Anthony Bourdain but is also loved by customers from every class. It has a loyal cult of customers. That customer loyalty is lucrative. An In-N-Out store outsells a typical McDonald's nearly twice over. In-N-Out's profit margin (measured by earnings before interest, taxes, depreciation, and amortization) is an estimated 20 percent.[5] That's higher than Shake Shack (16 percent) and other restaurant chains that typically own their locations, like Chipotle (10.5 percent).

Lynsi is a customer-centric leader and embodies W.A.Y.S. (see figure 5-3, page 97). She walks a mile in her employees' shoes, she asks for truth from associates, and she shows accountability by getting out of the office constantly. Just look at her Instagram and how she is constantly celebrating employees' birthdays and adding why she appreciates them so much. She also makes small improvements to the variables she can control.

She said, "Of course, connected and engaged *associates* do the best work in any company. We have very high standards, which means we have a lot of procedures and policies in place, but they only work when you have *associates* who are eager to follow them."

Snyder makes annual trips to her dad's ranch with employees—they play sports, learn in workshops, participate in team-building exercises, make films, and spend time together for what she calls In-N-Out family time. Of her employees, Snyder said, "They are the reason for our success, and they deserve to enjoy coming to work, to feel appreciated, and to be treated like family, which is what I consider them."

In-N-Out employees get competitive pay and career development. Restaurant workers in California make over nineteen dollars an hour, versus the nine or ten dollars or so that's typical at most national competitors, including McDonald's and Burger King.[6]

Like Trader Joe's, part- and full-time restaurant workers can enroll in dental, vision, and life insurance plans through the company, and full-timers can get health insurance and paid vacation. The average In-N-Out manager has been with the company for seventeen years and makes $163,000 annually, more than the typical California dentist, accountant, or financial adviser. Managers get profit-sharing too. "They're simulating an ownership mentality at the restaurant," says John Glass, a restaurant-industry equity analyst at Morgan Stanley. "That manager now has skin in the game."[7]

Lynsi and management spend a lot of time finding managers that are good with people. They know how important good leaders are to the culture of the company.

"We select leaders who are strong in the area of engaging associates in taking great care of our customers with great quality and service," she says. "They must also be able to create a team-oriented atmosphere, which is part of our mission statement."[8]

The company's mission is "about the quality, the friendliness, and the cleanliness. . . . We keep it simple." In-N-Out ranked highest on a survey by Market Force of burger chains.[9]

YOU CANNOT BLAME frontline employees for customer experiences. They don't have enough power to effect change other than an individual interaction with one customer. The guardrails and operational metrics are not set by them. There is no frontline employee who says, "The metric you're measuring us by is not creating customer-focused outcomes! We should change it!" It's up to the leader to be a coach, like Doc Rivers, or Lynsi Snyder, thinking about how to coach and manage the employees to get the right outcomes, including how success is measured and what the team stands for and what they don't stand for.

STORYTELLING WITH STYLE: MARY KAY ASH

Mary Kay Ash started her own company, Mary Kay Cosmetics, in 1963 with a $5,000 investment from her son. According to those who knew her, "Mary Kay was a very visible, very active role model: a hard-working, immaculately groomed mother of three who was doing everything within her power to see other women get ahead, and who loved mentoring so much that she referred to her saleswomen as her 'daughters.'"[10]

Mary Kay's saleswomen made more profit per unit than her competitors: a Mary Kay lipstick cost roughly double the price of competitive lipsticks and made twice the profit. Her home parties that sold the makeup was a genius marketing model because customers were targeted in intimate settings by trusted members of the community. Mary Kay made her company purposely inclusive, enabling her rapid expansion into Australia, South America, Europe, and Asia.

One day Mary was giving a talk to a group of salespeople. In the early years of Mary Kay Cosmetics, the company was growing rapidly but faced numerous challenges. Resources were stretched thin, and there was a constant push for innovation and new ideas to stay ahead of the competition. One day, during a company-wide meeting, she noticed a negative shift in the atmosphere. Employees seemed stressed and worried about meeting their targets, feeling the weight of the competitive industry. In response, Mary Kay talked about a bumblebee, which because of the rules of aerodynamic flight, technically shouldn't be able to fly. Its wings are too small, and its body is too heavy. But the bumblebee doesn't know these technical facts, so it flies anyway. She urged them not to be limited by what seems impossible but to strive for their goals despite the obstacles they might face.

She empathized with her employees, recognized the pressure they were under, and found a creative way to inspire and motivate them. In 2022, Mary Kay Cosmetics' revenue was $2.7 billion. How many bosses have you had that inspire, uplift, and encourage rather than using fear tactics and threats?

Mary Kay Ash embodied the customer experience mindset. As a leader she was also a coach, worrying always about the state of her employees. She used storytelling to inspire and took the time to care deeply about the employees who worked for her, not in a vain and lip service way, but in a genuine way. That's why, to this day, she has a very strong reputation and powerful legacy. And her company still exists today.

Like Mary Kay Ash, a customer-centric leader is approachable, and they want people at all levels of the organization to approach them should there be a problem or an opportunity or if they need help. Customer-centric leaders have the energy for influencing change. They have high amounts of positive energy—they smile a lot—because they genuinely love and believe in what they do. But they also smile knowing that when you smile you affect the people around you. And it's important to remember the impact you have on others with your attitude.

These individuals are making a difference in people's lives every day. These individuals are not easily thrown off track by challenges. They welcome the problems that arise when trying to do the best they can for employees and customers. The customer-centric leader has high integrity; team members believe these leaders and believe *in* these leaders. You can count on these leaders, full stop. There is no monkey business. They do what they say they're going to do. They have a high say-do ratio. Everyone trusts them a great deal.

STORYTELLING WITH STYLE: TRADER JOE'S

Trader Joe's employees just seem happy. This is one of the few retail stores left that have tons of people working there. I am a weekly customer and I never wait in line—the checkout process is very fast and efficient, unlike self-checkout. At Trader Joe's you can ask for a sample of any product that you see, and the playful atmosphere is reinforced by the unique art and signage at each store.

Joe Coulombe started Trader Joe's in 1967. Joe found many ways to bring difficult-to-find products at cheaper prices to customers. He was extremely clever. He brought to the mainstream almond butter, made out of the extra bits of almonds no one wanted to buy. In 1982, the United States had a quota on imported tuna. In 1981 in *Newsweek,* Coulombe read a story about a fish called pilchard, which tasted like tuna but was not. After a trip to Peru,

Coulombe realized the quality was just as good as tuna, so they packaged it, relabeled it as tuna, and cut the price.

There are dozens of stories like this on how Trader Joe's was able to provide incredibly low prices on hard-to-find products. Coulombe wrote that most grocers don't want to know where and how the food they sell is made, but his curiosity about this gave him a huge advantage. The products that Trader Joe's carries depend on the raw materials of the season, and if a material goes up in price, Trader Joe's might discontinue the product in order to not drive up the price to the customer. Trader Joe's is a company that has provided so much value to customers through the years that they avoided many technology innovations.

Trader Joe's *is* an experience. The stores are only eight to fifteen thousand square feet, a third of a typical grocery store. There are only eighteen kinds of pasta sauce compared with the dozens in most grocery stores; they prefer to not overwhelm the customer. The company operates a truck-to-shelf model, with no storage in the back, so the food doesn't sit, and all food is taken directly from the trucks and placed on the shelf. Because most of Trader Joe's foods are private labeled, the store has more control about many aspects of the food.

Every so often a company comes along and refuses to play by the rules that everyone else in the industry is operating under. For example, no self-checkout, no online ordering, no Instacart shopping, no app, no loyalty program, and very little marketing.

On the Trader Joe's podcast you can hear employees talk about why Trader Joe's makes decisions the way it does. They don't have a loyalty program because they believe customers are often the ones that foot the bill for a loyalty program, and they have no interest in treating some customers better than others.

Joe Coulombe once said, "Time and again I am asked why no one has successfully replicated Trader Joe's. The answer is that no one has been willing to pay the wages and benefits, and thereby attract—and keep—the quality of people who work at Trader Joe's."[11] There is poor customer service everywhere partially because of employee turnover, a result of poor employee experience, and employers do not want to compensate their customer-facing employees competitively. Arguably because they can't draw the link to an ROI.

Coulombe said his standard was simple: the average full-time employee in the stores would make the median family income for California. Back in those days it was about $7,000.[12] He also added that unions, a problem for some companies, weren't a problem for Trader Joe's because of the way he conducted employee feedback. Coulombe learned at his Stanford MBA program that employees never organized because of money: they organized because of unlistened-to grievances. He set up a program where the employee was interviewed by their boss's boss—a skip level from them. Coulombe said, "The principal purpose of this program was to vent grievances and address them where possible." He called it Letting Off Steam Equally. The company pays significantly higher still today than other grocers and also offers benefits. On Trader Joe's website it says the benefits include: medical, dental, and vision plans, paid time off, job growth based on performance, a 20 percent store discount, and a retirement plan.

The company wants the customer to come into the store because they believe shopping in the store is part of the experience. The discovery aspect of shopping is what makes Trader Joe's appealing. Many Trader Joe's don't have doors on their freezers to touch and look at the many varieties of frozen foods.[13] In 2022, when many companies were laying off employees, Trader Joe's opened new locations and hired twenty-four thousand new employees. Their retention is some of the highest in the industry. In 2015, Trader Joe's revenue was $8 billion. In 2022, Trader Joe's revenue was $13.3 billion.

The companies that understand that customer experience is a treasure chest have executives that go to the heart of where the work is happening.

Starbucks CEO Laxman Narasimhan shows his commitment to staying close to where the work is done by working one half-day a month as a barista. He said in a letter:

> To keep us close to the culture and our customers, as well as to our challenges and opportunities, I intend to continue working in stores . . . and I expect each member of the leadership team to also ensure our support centers stay connected and engaged in the realities of our stores for discussion and improvement.[14]

Another company that requires employees to play an active role in understanding the customer experience is DoorDash. Through its WeDash program, all salaried employees are required to deliver takeout, including CEO Tony Xu.[15] Delivering orders keeps Tony and all employees close to the customers to see their work in action. One disgruntled DoorDash employee ignited a nearly two thousand–comment thread on Blind, the anonymous professional social network. "What the actual f—k?" wrote an engineer with a reported total compensation of $400,000 a year. "I didn't sign up for this, there was nothing in the offer letter/job description about this." So not everyone has the customer experience mindset required and isn't up for the challenge.

The question you would have to ask yourself as a leader is if you would be comfortable with leaders that weren't willing to "flip burgers."

The most successful companies today have leaders that employees feel camaraderie with, that are genuinely interested in the experience of the customer (and the employee). Like Richard

Branson, who regularly rides his own airline and sits in the back of the airplane to mystery shop.

It has never been more important for executives to pretend they are on the TV show *Undercover Boss* every day. How many leaders are willing to be excited to work on the front lines to understand what employees go through and to know the bottlenecks in the business? While many airline CEOs fly their planes to see the crew in action, Air New Zealand's CEO, Greg Foran, takes leadership one step further—he regularly joins the cabin crew and serves snacks.[16] He believes the best way to understand his customers and employees is to be right in the action and join them in the work.

The most customer-centric leaders are setting an example by frequently spending time with frontline workers. Customer-focused companies are led by executives that don't create distance between themselves and where the customer-facing work happens.

Another example comes from the CEO of Waste Management, Jim Fish. Jim started attending the team meetings of the employees that take the trash out, even though they met at 3:00 a.m. By working alongside employees, and going to the same meetings, Jim builds camaraderie with his team. He learns unique insights into their struggles.

When COVID hit on a Sunday morning, Jim called an emergency meeting. Many of his fifty thousand employees worked in the tristate area and New York City, the epicenter of the COVID epidemic. He was honest with his team that he was just as terrified as everyone else. But he guaranteed them they would not miss a paycheck, and he would figure out a way to continue paying them for forty hours a week of work. Jim Fish is a customer-centric CEO. Five years ago stock was $83, now it's $173.80 (December 1, 2023).

STORYTELLING WITH STYLE:
OSCAR MUNOZ, FORMER COO, CSX;
FORMER CEO, UNITED AIRLINES

CSX routinely ranked at the bottom of the US railroads for operational efficiency, safety, and profitability. Munoz wrote in his book *Turnaround Time*, "Heavily investing in workers' experience and well-being was considered by Wall Street as 'nice to have.' . . . Bucking that conventional wisdom, we made it a priority, and it became the basis of our turnaround success." His goal was to win back the trust of the railroad workers. He took the same approach while at United Airlines a few years later, personally spending time with employees and customers. With this employee-focused approach at CSX, Munoz improved operating income by a whopping 600 percent. Their story is what is known as a "Cinderella story." In sports, the terms *Cinderella story* and *Cinderella team* are used to refer to situations in which competitors achieve far greater success than would reasonably have been best expected.

When I interviewed Munoz three years after he retired from United Airlines as CEO, he noted that the worst position you can put your frontline employees in is to be the face of a broken experience. When Munoz came to United, many employees told him they were just tired of apologizing. In our interview, when I asked him what's the best thing an airline could do to be customer centric, he answered the airline needs to be efficient—the flights need to run on time, and no amount of free snacks or filet mignon and champagne is going to fix that. Customer experience transformations can feel like getting your pipes cleaned. No one on the outside will notice that it happened, but everything will be flowing better. An investment in customer experience can just be a huge upgrade to operations and employee experience, so employees feel proud to represent the brand.

STORYTELLING WITH STYLE: INDRA NOOYI, PEPSI

Consider Indra Nooyi, the former CEO of Pepsi. One day when Indra was CEO, she went back to India to visit her mom. Her mom wanted Indra to dress up and sit with her as Indra's mom's friends, neighbors, and cousins came over to visit. To Indra's surprise, all the guests ignored her; in fact, they didn't even say hello. They simply went to her mom and said, "You brought up such a good kid." In that moment it occurred to Indra to consider her own employees' parents—the importance of parents feeling proud of their kids and what that meant for the kid—because even Indra was the child of someone. Indra started personally writing handwritten letters to the parents of the twenty-nine senior executives on her executive staff.

She said, "I tell the parents what a great job their son or daughter is doing. That recognition is worth more than money, stock runs, hugs, tickets—anything—because at the end of the day, when your parents say to you, 'I'm so proud of you; your boss just wrote to me saying you're awesome,' the look on their face is worth more than one million dollars."[17]

Under her leadership, PepsiCo's revenue grew from $35 billion in 2006 to $63.5 billion in 2017, and by the end of 2017, total shareholder return was 162 percent.[18]

All of the examples in this book cite companies that understand how important the employee experience is to building a customer experience. From Doc Rivers who embraced Ubuntu and led the Celtics to be 2008 World Champions, to Amy Shore's internal feedback system, to Lynsi Snyder at In-N-Out Burger, to Mary Kay Ash, to Indra Nooyi and the handwritten letters she wrote to parents, to the way Trader Joe's compensates its staff competitively, to Oscar Munoz's focus on frontline staff at CSX and later at United Airlines, the path to a customer-focused culture is an employee-focused culture.

EXERCISE

When was the last time you asked employees what it was like to work at your company?

How often do you ask employees what would make their jobs better?

How would employees rate the experience of working at your company, and what could your company do better?

What can you personally do better as a manager or a colleague?

What kind of internal engagement program do you have in your contact center?

What is one thing you could be doing for the employee experience that you're not doing now?

9

Law 7: Evaluate Success and Measure What Can Be Measured

Relationships are both art and science, but they are more art than science—and the way we manage and measure business today doesn't account for this. The discussion of metrics is one of the more polarizing topics for leaders that run contact centers. The predominant metric for customer experience today is Net Promoter Score (NPS), which is how likely a customer is to recommend a company to a friend on a scale of 0 to 10. The NPS puts respondents into three categories: "promoters," who provide ratings of 9 or 10; "passives," who provide ratings of 7 or 8; and "detractors," who provide ratings of 0 to 6. The Net Promoter Score results from a calculation that involves subtracting the percentage of detractors from the percentage of promoters collected by the survey.

But NPS is problematic. And with the proliferation of data today and the ability to plow through millions of pieces of structured and unstructured data, NPS for many leaders is losing the appeal it once had. The minute you bring up NPS to practitioners, you face problems. Bryan Sander, head of customer experience for AAA, told me, "I have watched people get into 'religious wars' about whether or not to use NPS, and I don't like what it does to the human beings who are in the debate." NPS is the predominant metric for measuring customer experience, but there are a lot of problems with it on its own.

I had a client in the construction and homebuilding space. At the end of the year, the divisions with the highest performing NPS earned a trip with the CEO to Martha's Vineyard. To get that carrot, a few of the division presidents cheated. They would wine and dine customers to get the high score. What is the point of NPS if it's just a lie so everyone can sleep at night? Relationships take work, and if there is no honest pulse check on how those relationships are going, that's a problem.

You are in relationships in your own life. These relationships can be very fulfilling, but they are also at times taxing. When you give to other people, it can be exhausting, resource draining, and even frustrating at times. But that's life! And if you want people to care about you and help you in a time of need, you have to do that for others. It's the same for your customers; if you do not fulfill your end of the contract with your customers, they will leave.

The good news is now there is a lot of great technology to assist in the management of customer relationships, but the problem for most companies is not the technology—the problem is the goal setting, the way contact centers are managed. The goal should not be serving the greatest amount of customers in the cheapest way possible; you need to give a lot of thought to what it feels like to be not only on the receiving end of the experience but to be the person delivering an underfunded experience.

But businesses often have so many customers that they can abuse customers and for a little while not notice, until customers find something better and they start leaving in droves. If customers do business with you only because they have to—and you are the only option—you will soon be disrupted. The only thing that differentiates you is the health of your relationships and the trust you build by consistently being there for customers. You must focus on their well-being at all times and what is best for them. The truth is you can't afford not to.

Why in business have leaders become very two dimensional? If it's not 100 percent clear something will make them money, they won't do it. In life we know that investing in relationships will enrich the relationship—our reputation—and the quality of life overall. So why in business—in particular the contact center—are we so blindsided?

For example, many start-ups don't make money for years while they invest in customer-centric products and experiences. The incredible music streaming service Spotify has 517.69 million active users worldwide with approximately 229 million premium subscribers. Spotify, launched in 2006, is just recently becoming profitable in 2023. Netflix, launched in 1998, didn't become profitable for eight years. Jeff Bezos infamously said he felt early on no one understood what Amazon was going to be, but by focusing on "building the world's most customer-centric company," he earned a place in the lives of customers globally. It begs the question, "What does success look like, and how do you know how to measure it?"

There are so many colloquialisms about measurement. "What's measured gets improved." Or, "If you measure it, you will treasure it." But the contact center exposes how much or how little the company cares about its customer relationships. The way a company manages its contact center—or any customer-facing role—says everything about what they prioritize. The management of the contact center can be very complicated, but when you get very clear about your goal, the path is clear.

What you measure as a business says everything about what you care about and everything about your culture. At the end of 2001, Enron was exposed for inflating their success. Their reported financial condition was sustained by an institutionalized, systematic, and creatively planned accounting fraud. Did they understand the magnitude and corruption of what they were doing? Many companies are lying to themselves every day about the health of their business and their customer relationships. But when companies and individuals start working toward a more efficient process of measurement of success, based on reality and real tangible goals, everything gets better! So many great leaders understand that a commitment to the truth, to reality, is the best metric.

If there was one glaring problem with customer experience, it's this: performance metrics are the number one hindrance to creating a customer-focused culture and organization. How you measure success says everything about what your company values and everything about how hard you are willing to work to make improvements based on the reality of the customer feedback, not a euphemistic view from someone that simply wants to keep their job and make their bonus.

It's relevant for people as individuals as well. In life you must decide what you are not to figure out what you are. People are a by-product of what measurements they hold themselves to. If a person is so fixated on a metric that they will lie to themselves to achieve it, they are engaging in a dysfunctional pattern of behavior that will prevent them from achieving actual growth. It's the same for businesses. Figuring out how to measure your own success is one of the biggest decisions you will ever make in your life. It involves questions like "What do I want for myself?" "How do I know if I've lived a good life?" "What do I value?" "What do I care about?" and "What do I want the outcome to look like?"

If a leader is incentivized by money or recognition (or just keeping their job) to meet a metric set for them that isn't customer centric, then it makes sense that this leader would do what they had to do to meet that metric.

This is a time of extreme flux and change in contact centers. The rise of digital technologies and mounting pressure and expectations from customers, all coupled with a legacy attitude toward the contact center as a cost center, leaves customer experience leaders frustrated. They feel left with too little to accomplish what they want and little respect for what they do. The metric for the contact center is often to do the most amount of work with the smallest budget possible. For the companies that do this—what a missed opportunity! And for the companies that invest in their contact centers—they are sprinting ahead of the competition.

It's not just B2C companies that struggle with how to operationalize the nurturing of customer relationships; it's also B2B. Habits from COVID have left the customer in the dust, with many employees used to not having to travel to meet customers. Like at one large consulting firm where the CEO told me that his teams are used to the comfort of working at home in their pajamas, and he's having trouble getting them back out to spend time with clients. They are too comfortable with Zoom, and the customer relationship has taken a toll. Dinners, golf outings, concerts, and coffees where advisers would build relationships with clients are a thing of the past, and too many employees simply don't want to leave their house. They don't want to have to invest time in building the relationship anymore. His ask of me seemed reasonable, and I genuinely wanted to help him fix his culture. However, upon meeting this group in person and speaking with many of them directly, I soon discovered how tired and overworked these consultants were. They were already working seventy-hour weeks, and were too tired to pretend they enjoyed going above and beyond to wine and dine customers on top of their current load. The CEO did not want to recognize he was living in a fantasy world about what employees are capable of when they are already exhausted. When I asked the CEO how much time he spent inspiring, engaging, and developing the partners of his company who could drive this culture, I was shocked to hear the answer was almost zero. He wanted to create a culture at his company, but not if it meant he had to eat his own dog food. Ultimately, in the four-hour workshop I ran for his top 250 leaders, he was unhappy. He said he was unhappy that I gave the employees breaks instead of simply going straight through the four hours, which is what he said he normally does. He wanted a customer culture that he didn't create with his employees first. Can you force employees to spend more time with customers and care more? You cannot force employees to do much if they don't want to. If you simply want to invest a client-focused culture out of thin air, but you have none of the programs or processes in place to make that happen, it's not going to happen. First you have to create a culture by putting performance metrics in place that are supported by an employee-centric culture based on reality. People are human beings, and if your vision is not rooted in the reality, you won't be able to achieve what you say you want to. Whether you're creating a customer-centric consulting firm, or a contact center, a discussion about culture is a discussion about metrics. The metrics determine everything, but they must be supported by a culture that won't set employees up to fail.

Stephanie Shaffer De Jesús has been consulting for a pharma company that has 150,000 employees and $100 billion in revenue in the fiscal year ending in June 2023. She helps brands create metrics with Experience Level Agreements, also known as XLAs (normally Service Level Agreements). XLAs are a way to run your contact center that starts with the customer experience and backs into the metric. Most contact centers don't do this. They don't think of the outcome they want from a customer experience perspective and work backward. Contact center metrics are guardrails, but they don't offer the business intelligence to fuel process improvement, tell the story, isolate root causes, and ultimately transform the business like XLA metrics do.

Stephanie believes some of the most trusted brands and global companies measure the same standard metrics that they have measured for decades. She says, "Most of these metrics tie to contractual obligations and stick to the old adage 'What gets measured gets managed' and manage the basics. This is strictly an outside view looking inward approach with a heavy focus on operations." XLAs revolve around the customer's core expectations. By backing into your XLA by understanding what the customer values, rather than the SLA, you glean the true root of loyalty and figure out how to drive a metrics campaign that deepens the connection customers have with the brand. Additionally, if you are a company that cares about employee experience, then this customer-centric approach to building a metrics program also improves the employee experience, and vice versa.

According to this approach, one or several metrics are often looked at as the end-all-be-all indicator of the health of the business. If they are within a certain threshold deemed as "acceptable," then there is no focus on any further opportunities and no deeper dive into the voice of the customer data. Voice of the customer data is exactly how it sounds—it's what the data tells you about what the customer is actually going through. This is gathered from surveys, social media, comments, and other forms of feedback. In contact center language, practitioners call their metric the "satisfaction goal." For example, they might say "my satisfaction is at 95 percent; I am above goal." This score is extracted from the Customer Satisfaction score, automated in all customer experience platforms and watched as a main metric. But what the contact center leader doesn't realize is there is still work to do. What about the 5 percent that are not happy? And this is in a rosy scenario. Many contact centers don't have high customer satisfaction to begin with.

If you want to create a new metrics program based on Experience Level Agreements, you can do the following:

1. **Understand your brand promise and how you can best bring it to life.** What do customers expect of your brand? What essential part do you play in their lives? What is your differentiator? Keep

these answers in mind when you construct the XLAs. Are you delivering your brand promise consistently?

2. **How do you connect with your customers on a deep, emotional level?** After the brand promise, explore what emotions your service provokes. Does it calm, soothe, offer peace of mind, give a competitive advantage, excite, exude confidence? Keep those emotions and feelings close because they are the connection and will be included in the XLA questions. The psychology of your brand promise goes deeper than surface level. Are you meeting emotional needs to keep customers coming back?

3. **What do your customers want?** This is the time for deep data analysis of the *voice* of your customer. This can be done by leveraging multichannel contacts at various listening posts. For example, analyzing feedback via text analytics (solicited), analyzing call interactions (unsolicited), and a social media component (Google locations review, unsolicited). What are your customers repeatedly asking for and what topics are commonly called out?

From here you create a quadrant and tell the story of your customer's core expectations. Map these expectations to current questions on your survey and analytics engine or create new survey questions (and retire former ones that don't directly connect to actionable insights) that roll up directly to the XLA metric. Include the emotion and brand promise throughout in a clear and understandable way to "tell the story." When you evangelize the XLAs in your organization, it brings alignment to all regarding what is owned by all employees to meet customer core expectations. Eventually, as you integrate it into the culture, it becomes a refreshing mantra of what the customer needs that will ensure that you are a true and steadfast advocate for your customers.

An example of an XLA for a bank may be "Help Me," "Know Me," "Value Me," "Protect Me." This is what customers expect from their bank. An example for an IT organization may be "Make It Fast," "Make It Friendly," "Make It Easy," "Get It Resolved" (see figure 9-1). After you map these to current survey questions—or create new ones—it's time for A/B testing. This is the time to gather a baseline and prioritize which XLA moves into production first.

FIGURE 9-1

When you are ready to put XLAs into action, leadership needs to honestly answer:

How far are you willing to go to empower your support staff to bring these metrics to life?

The benefit of using XLAs is that you constantly analyze customer sentiment, which fuels continuous improvement and a deeper understanding of what customers want.

The XLAs are the behind-the-scenes direct-impact to your customer to see if the core competencies are being met or not. Future-forward organizations are saying goodbye to metrics-only management. They are marrying XLA management with customer sentiment to understand their customers' needs and fuel continuous improvement. This approach adds more depth to a voice of the customer program and accelerates the speed to business transformation.

By reverse engineering the customer's core expectations and backing into XLAs, you can do a deep analysis of voice of the customer data indicating expectations, the brand promise, and the deep, emotional connection. These things can be interwoven into metrics to accurately measure if the organization is truly providing what was promised to customers.

When you analyze customer sentiment via AI tools like Text Analytics, you can see numerous layers deeper at an accelerated rate. You can see at a high level how a customer "feels" about a brand. You can continue to drill down into people, process, and technology as root causes and understand customer pain points as well as moments of delight. This allows you to take the signals, understand the insights, and inspire action in a consistent and agile process.

EARNED GROWTH RATE

There is also a very basic way to look at customer happiness. You can obviously look at sales. If your sales are high, that means you are doing something right, but you don't know if what you are selling is so good the customer will come back. A better metric than just "sales" is how many of those customers are so happy they tell their friends. It sounds simple, but it turns out it's not that easy to track. At least according to Fred Reichheld, Bain consultant, NPS creator, and author of the book *Winning on Purpose*.

I have interviewed Fred Reichheld twice and talked to him about his new version of NPS called Earned Growth Rate (EGR). EGR tracks the growth a company earns through repeat purchases and customer referrals. For instance, a company like Apple might have a high EGR due to its loyal customers who not only make repeat purchases but also refer the brand to their friends and family. According to Reichheld, in simple terms, Earned Growth Rate is understanding how many of your new customers arrive as a referral from current customers. This can be hard to track unless you are a membership-based company because the company does not always ask how the new customers came in. If you are Costco, and all customers have a membership ID, this gets easier. EGR is popular with subscription-based software companies.

If you do use NPS, there are some tips from Bryan Sander of AAA on how to do it carefully. According to Bryan, missteps include relying solely on NPS without any context. This means that relying solely on the NPS score by itself is "thin" data. You can supplement the thin data by also looking at other qualitative research: customer calls, focus groups, direct observation, or user testing.

Employees can game the system in many different ways to try to increase scores, especially if their performance or compensation is tied to NPS. Bryan recommends clearly setting expectations that employees should avoid gaming the system, putting automation in place that flags anomalies in NPS score data that may have been caused by gaming. Also, be careful of incentive plans that include NPS scores as a payout metric. One idea Bryan also has is to have a cross-functional, executive-level customer experience steering committee that is accountable for deeply understanding customer feedback, prioritizing improvements based on that feedback, and executing the improvements.

There are so many great ways to understand what is happening with your customers other than using NPS surveys, like using data and analytics to drill down to what is happening with customers and doing root-cause analysis. The scoreboard can become a problem because it distracts leaders from what will be necessary to achieve sustainable and continued growth.

Many businesses have taken customer experience and applied stats that are no longer relevant. Customer experience leaders are missing the point and have lost their way in focusing on a scoreboard that isn't guiding a customer-centric strategy. And so many leaders are so excited by data that they never actually take the time to talk with customers or frontline employees. The data will never be as accurate, insightful, or powerful as what you hear from the customer's mouth.

Why don't we think of the contact center as a place where employees contribute to the bottom line? Business until now has been very black and white: "You work in sales, so you make the company money." "You work in service, so you cost the company money!" Everyone at your company touches the customer experience in some way whether you acknowledge it or not.

Customers are more prone to come back after a contact center agent can actually help them, more than if they see an advertisement interrupting their favorite TV show.

THE CHALLENGE WITH
CONTACT CENTER SCORECARDS

I recently met with a client, a medium-sized membership association that also sells insurance. I was working with them on a keynote presentation to their contact center advisers. The client told me how frustrated they were with their contact center agents. He said, "These agents have zero confidence," "They just don't know how to sell!" and "They don't ask probing questions." And "They just do the bare minimum—solve the customer's problem—and don't do any sales." It was interesting to me to hear this initial frustration from management. I thought, are they just hiring the wrong type of agents to speak with customers? They were using a Bain "integrity selling" and "asking formula." The formula I saw on the paper was extremely complicated and confusing. While being a likable person, the agent had to jump all over the page ensuring their words matched what the company was asking them to do. It was a tall order for anyone, even the most skilled speaker.

My client wrote me in an email, "Our advisers, through a service approach, are great at being polite and making statements, but they *struggle* asking open-ended questions to find and fill needs. They were groomed for the last couple of years to be polite, professionals in their job." The company had a complicated scorecard and wordy scripts to measure each agent. The scorecard would measure every action and word. For example, a member calls in to cancel. The adviser (by requirement of their scorecard) asks a couple questions in an attempt to save the sale. The member ultimately cancels. The adviser receives a successful score because they "checked the boxes" on those attempts.

I asked to see this scorecard and immediately noticed how complicated it was—it had nine different areas that rated the agent on four different levels from minor to moderate to major to critical. While the company says they do not use any kind of "script" with agents, if they don't hit the many words and recommendations on the scorecard, the agent fails. When I met the team on-site and I asked one of the lower-level managers about it, she winked at me and told me she didn't really use it. Creating scorecards that are so frustrating that managers skip them is not a good practice, because then you do not have uniformity across your culture.

The challenge with scorecards is people forget you are dealing with people—and there is variation. In the contact center, leaders cannot always control everything. You can't tell an agent "Use your best judgment" but also throw an impossible scorecard at them. If the agent is judged by a scorecard, even if there is no script, the agent will not be able to listen to the customer. The agent becomes so self-conscious about the scorecard, they can't perform at the highest level. The best approach is to hire people that like people, give them tools to do their jobs, and measure them in a way that drives customer-focused outcomes.

The contradiction is also with the two groups measuring the agent by different standards. The company on the one hand wants the contact center agents to feel comfortable improving on the spot and getting to know what the customer actually needs so they can upsell and cross-sell them. But at the same time, the quality team (separate from the contact center manager) is holding them to a long and tedious scorecard. I told my client that if he would just remove the quality scorecard, sales would increase.

Management listened to my recommendations. When I checked on my client a few months later, he told me they were in the process of integrating an entirely new quality assurance structure. They killed their scorecards and checklists and freed up the advisers to have more organic conversations. They still have KPI expectations with weights aimed at a balanced service with voice of the customer, efficiency, and business growth, but the feedback provided by QA is more aligned with service and suggestions on how to capitalize on opportunities. They no longer focus on deducting points because an agent failed to mention mandated talking points. The rollout is a collaboration between the contact center manager and the QA teams. Advisers are providing feedback as they dial in the finished product.

The importance of metrics in shaping a successful customer experience strategy cannot be overstated. Monitoring the right customer experience metrics allows teams to gauge the effectiveness of their strategies, identify areas for improvement, and continually enhance the customer experience.

One of the significant hurdles for customer experience teams is demonstrating the impact of their initiatives to secure support from executives and other departments. Metrics serve as a compelling tool in this regard, substantiating the value of customer experience efforts and the importance of fostering strong customer relationships for the business's bottom line. According to the previously mentioned survey I conducted of a thousand business leaders with DDI, 30 percent of respondents are not tracking cost savings or revenue generated in the contact center, which puts these leaders in a precarious position to get any further resources for their programs.[1]

Metrics also reveal opportunities for growth and enable teams to continually refine their customer experiences. In an era where customers wield more power and exhibit less brand loyalty, utilizing metrics to improve and stay competitive is crucial for retaining customers and remaining relevant.

But traditional metrics like Net Promoter Score and Customer Satisfaction score that many brands relied on in the past may not fully capture the expectations of today's sophisticated customers. The more modern companies are using data and analytics to get the full picture, picking up where the other metrics lack substance. These other metrics often overlook critical aspects of the customer experience or fail to delve into the root of customers' expectations.

Companies need to elevate their metric monitoring and track new behaviors and attitudes. As we mentioned earlier in the book, practitioners like Naomi Wheeless from Square understand that contact center leaders should manage the contact center like a product manager would. This makes sense considering the experience is, in fact, a product. They need to constantly be looking at ways to not only capture the full story of the customer experience in the contact center but find compelling ways to tell that story, which will create more resources for the contact center. This is where ensuring senior executives dive into the qualitative data really helps.

Although 82 percent of customer experience leaders expect their budgets to increase this year, Forrester suggests that these numbers may be overly optimistic given the fragility of budgets during a recession, and we can't predict what is coming tomorrow. For a period, you might have to do more with less and do so in a crafty manner. But some of the most successful entrepreneurs started their businesses with very little resources, like Mary Kay Ash and David Geffen. Creativity will serve contact center leaders today who often are faced with mounting problems and don't always have the support from upper management to solve them. If you think of your customer experience as a product, and your role as a product manager, than you can also think of yourself as an entrepreneur. Imagine if Jeff Bezos ran your contact center. What would it look like?

The entire business world is a pendulum, swinging from efficiency to effectiveness, according to Daniel Hong, former VP and research director for Digital Customer and Collaboration at Forrester (see figure 9-2). Daniel is now the chief marketing officer for Minerva CQ, a generative AI software company (which I serve on the advisory board of). I met Daniel in 2007 when he was my friend's boss at Ovum, an analyst firm. He managed a team of analysts, and I was starting out my career in the contact center world in New York City. For the contact center, you need both efficiency and effectiveness. The pendulum will swing toward effectiveness during good economic times and efficiency during bad economic times. Daniel came up with this idea in collaboration with Ian Jacobs when they were both at Ovum. Ian is currently a VP and research director of customer experience at Forrester.

From Efficiency to Effectiveness

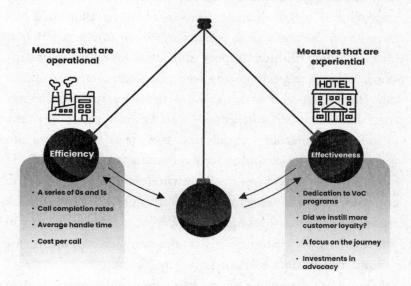

FIGURE 9-2

Daniel told me recently in a conversation, "Efficiency is when you're looking at the contact center from an operational perspective. They're hard numbers like call completion rates, average handle time, and call wait times. Measures that are operational—these are of an efficient environment like a factory." But he said you don't just want to be efficient; you want to be effective. Effectiveness is when you have taken your customer strategy beyond the basics. It's looking at the voice of the customer, constantly looking at improvements, and having a line of sight and if we meet those needs, above and beyond. Did we instill more customer loyalty? Effectiveness is the investment in customer retention and advocacy. But the impulse when the economy goes bad is to cave into the tremendous pressure to reduce costs.

For example, Bryan Sander, the current head of customer experience for AAA, remembers when he worked at Inuit in the early 2000s. Intuit, a B2B financial software company, pioneered Net Promoter Score and was an early mover in customer experience. He said, "I was running support and service for one of their divisions. We were experimenting with outsourcing and customer care. There were a lot of factors we were solving for, and one was cost." He remembers when they decided to offshore some of the technical customer support calls to save money. After the program was taken live, the customers were very unhappy. Sander said, "At first we were assured by our vendor who told us that the negative customer feedback was simply initial turbulence." The feedback stayed consistent, with scoring and verbatims. He said, "If you were to chart out customer satisfaction with tech support, there's a dramatic difference sustained over time."

He realized they had a big problem and went to the executive team and said, "We know on paper this is saving us money, but here's what our customers are consistently saying, based on a high volume of surveys." They played the executive team the recorded calls and together made the decision to pull the offshore program back to the US. After that, their customer satisfaction scores improved. The lesson he learned from his time at Intuit is you have to tread carefully when you are looking to automate or take calls out of the call center in order to realize savings. He added, "Things might go unnoticed that will catch up to you." He said, on his own middle management team, they saw the problem and wanted to find out if everyone saw the situation the same way. They had to undo a decision that was saving millions of dollars, and he said that took courage. He believes contact center leaders will be rewarded for doing the right thing for the customer "even if there are tough innings." He added that courage is a leadership requirement, especially in a customer experience initiative.

"There is an art to customer experience. It's a living, breathing thing you have to nurture every day," said Daniel Hong. "You need the mindshare and to win the hearts of customers—the front line matters." Daniel believes mindshare is when your customers think of great service, they think of your brand. Or when customers think of your brand, they think of great service.

Daniel advises leaders to manage contact center staff as human beings and team members, not as call center workers. Daniel advises that it's normal to have ups and downs, but the important thing is to be generally trending in the right direction.

If you knew that your customer-facing agents were the most important people at your company—because they get the special and impactful opportunity to talk to customers—what resources would you put toward their employee experience? How would you measure them differently or manage them differently?

The first part of any management strategy is to think about your goals. Take the time to get together with your colleagues, and think about what you care about. What are the behaviors you want to drive? The performance metrics are the most important aspect of your business—these metrics will determine what is made a priority at the company and how employees and managers know they did their jobs. If you are on the board of the company, the metric you set for your CEO will determine the metrics they set for their senior team, resulting in a cascade of metrics. If you want a customer-focused company but you only look at quarterly sales, you will not drive the right behavior. Metrics big and small matter, every single day. They matter at the top and they matter at the bottom.

EXERCISE

Answer the following:

What are your contact center goals? Do the metrics match the goals? If you didn't worry about the status quo in the contact center, would you still use the same metrics?

If you viewed the contact center as a critical part of a customer acquisition and retention strategy, how would the metrics be different?

Consider the XLA process discussed previously. If you moved from simply SLAs to XLAs, what would that process look like for you and who would be involved?

Who would need to be on your performance goals task force, and who would you bring in to have a discussion about a completely new way to think about your customer-facing initiatives, including your contact center?

10

Law 8: Reaffirm the Priority: Keep Customer Experience Front and Center

Most companies are bad at customer experience because it is really hard to do. Not only is it hard to get started, but it's hard to keep it up. Changing economic conditions, changing priorities, and changes in leadership and personnel—how is any corporation supposed to stay the course over years and years, decades and decades?

What business leaders might feel is very far away could be right at their fingertips. Just like a person, a business can change; they just have to want to.

When you talk about customer experience, it is a series of high-level business decisions. But it is also how you manage your employees. And it is definitely how you set up and manage your contact center.

To quote Peloton instructor Jess Sims, "How you do anything is how you do everything." Customer experience is a decision you make every single day, and everything affects the customer experience. For example, what does your leadership team look like? Or in the words of Kelly McDonald, whom I interviewed about her book *Crafting the Customer Experience for People Not Like You*, you have to be willing to understand your own limitations and hire people that do not have the same background as you. In this book I've talked a lot about being a self-aware leader—being aware of what you know—but also being just as self-aware about what you don't know.

Customer experience is like exercising. You have to do it all the time or you lose your muscle. Being customer-focused is a way of life.

STORYTELLING WITH STYLE: GLOSSIER

In an industry where customers have long been told what products they need by big makeup companies, Glossier's customer-focused mindset is unique. Their success shows how much customers want brands to listen to them. Chief Operating Officer Henry Davis says, "Before we even make anything, we make it because we learned from our customers what they are missing, both from a brand and a product perspective, that will make their lives better."[1]

A makeup and skin care brand that customers would actually want to wear on a sweatshirt—that was the goal behind creating Glossier. Build a brand that customers are so obsessed with that they can't help sharing it with friends, family, and even strangers.

And it worked: today, an incredible 70 percent of Glossier's online sales and traffic come from peer-to-peer referrals.[2]

Much of Glossier's success comes from flipping the model and mindset of traditional makeup companies on its head. Instead of selling only makeup, Glossier focuses on skin care with the mission "Skin first. Makeup second."

In 2014, founder Emily Weiss raised $10.4 million and officially launched Glossier with just four products: moisturizer, face mist, skin tint, and lip balm. From the beginning, customers could tell there was something different about the brand: everything from the marketing and product design to the online experience felt fresh and accessible to customers.

If a company could sell you two products, even though you only needed one, why would they say anything?

One of Glossier's bestsellers is its innovative Milky Jelly cleanser, which came from customers sharing the frustration with needing two products to wash their face: makeup remover and face wash. Glossier simplified the process by combining the products into a single product for an innovative dual-wash face wash. On the outside, it would cost a company money to sell the customer less product, but this is a move to build trust with the customer. By doing what is best for the customer, you do what is best for the relationship. Other brands might be worried about cutting their sales in half by combining products, but Glossier was totally focused on meeting customers' needs. "We innovate and develop products to meet those needs directly because we understand what they are."[3]

Today, Glossier has more than $180 million in annual revenue and a cult following, and customers happily wear the brand on a sweatshirt.

STORYTELLING WITH STYLE: BARKBOX

Another example of differentiating on service and personalization is BarkBox, a dog product subscription service company that comes with two treats, two toys, and a chew. The products are exclusive to BarkBox and fit a monthly theme. Taking things to the next level is BarkBox's amazing attention to personalization. Of the one million boxes it sends out each month, there are around 120,000 different varieties based on the size and breed of the dog and things like allergies. Personalization also comes in the form of tailoring boxes to meet an individual dog's needs. The BarkBox team makes an effort to talk to as many customers as possible, which usually ends up being around one-third of its customers each month.

From those interactions, the company's Happy Team, which focuses on customer experience, created the No Dog Left Behind program. If a customer calls in with a certain request for a product, the team goes out of its way to make it happen. At one point the team had twenty thousand boxes going out every month, each one hand-assembled with notes of the customer's request. One customer didn't want pork treats in the BarkBox for her pig, so the team handmade her a box with treats for pigs. Other customers called wanting toys that could withstand their aggressive chewer dogs, so BarkBox made a new line of products and put them in those customers' individual boxes. The company has since built technology to match the needs of the team and customers and to scale the personalization process.

The founder of the company, Henrik Werdelin, gives the same advice you heard at the beginning of the book from Tricia Griffith: "Do things that don't scale." It seems counterintuitive to business success, but customers rarely get these bespoke customer experiences, so if you provide them, the customer will be very happy.

Companies often want to create big systems to solve problems en masse, but customers are unique. The best solutions happen when a company and its employees have empathy and think of what's best for each individual customer. Most brands can do something manually for a long time before coming up with a scalable solution. BarkBox answers its customer emails individually to gain insight and build strong customer relationships. Personalization is the root of BarkBox's success. Paying attention to individual needs and taking the time to not only listen to customers but to go above and beyond to meet their needs make a difference. By putting customers and their dogs first and making their lives easier and better, BarkBox has secured loyal customers—both humans and canines.

Think about it. What is one thing you could start doing that would resonate with the customer, even if it did not scale perfectly?

Customer experience is not about only the customer, and it's not even purely about the company; customer experience is about *you*. Living the customer-focused life is living a life of service. You must take care of yourself because other people depend on you, but you must then help others. That's the definition of a leader. Customer experience is a way of life; it's a mindset. Customer experience is about putting in the work. It's about believing in yourself and doing things that are hard. Seeing what you are made of and what you are capable of is what makes life meaningful. You have to fight for the things you care about. Life is about the struggle. The meaning is in the ups and downs, in the losses and victories, but it's also about leaving nothing on the mat.

There is so much work to be done in the world. We need all the helpers we can get. Being a customer-focused person is really about healing the world. The faster we embrace being uncomfortable, the sooner we can fix some of the systemic issues that plague the world. The customer experience mindset is a way of life—it's living a life of meaning through service to others. And it's not just good for your customer, it's not just good for the business, it's good for you. Being in service to others means you have purpose in your life every day, and that meaning makes for a happier and more fulfilling life. I believe in the transformative power of customer experience, and I believe in you.

Now that we have gone through CX LEADER together, you can work on your own scorecard and see how you perform.

CUSTOMER-CENTRIC
LEADERSHIP SCORECARD

CREATE A CUSTOMER EXPERIENCE MINDSET.

Criteria:

Employees regularly undergo training on customer experience.

Leaders prioritize customer feedback in decision-making.

There's a clear communication channel for customers to share
   experiences.

Score (1–10): ____

EXCEED LONG-TERM PROFIT EXPECTATIONS.

Criteria:

There's a balance in investments for short-term and long-term
goals.

Financial growth aligns with customer satisfaction metrics.

Prioritize value to customer in pricing strategies.

Score (1–10): ____

LAY OUT YOUR CUSTOMER EXPERIENCE
STRATEGY AND STICK TO IT.

Criteria:

Have a documented customer experience strategy.

Regularly review strategy effectiveness.

Flexibly adapt strategy based on customer feedback, while
   staying true to core objectives.

Score (1–10): ____

EMBARK ON YOUR NINETY-DAY GET-STARTED PLAN.

Criteria:

Clear milestones set for the first ninety days.

Achieve early wins in customer experience improvements.
Establish a feedback loop within the first ninety days.

Score (1–10): ____

ANTICIPATE THE FUTURE BY BEING
A CUSTOMER EXPERIENCE FUTURIST.

Criteria:

Regularly analyze industry trends and innovations.

Proactive measures adapt to anticipated customer needs.

Customer experience strategy accounts for future market
shifts.

Score (1–10): ____

DON'T FORGET THAT EMPLOYEES ARE CUSTOMERS TOO.

Criteria:

Employee feedback is actively sought and valued.

Programs are in place for employee experience and well-being.

Employee satisfaction is aligned with customer satisfaction.

Score (1–10): ____

EVALUATE SUCCESS AND MEASURE WHAT CAN BE MEASURED.

Criteria:

Create key performance indicators for customer experience.

Regularly review customer-centric metrics.

Have a continuous feedback loop with customers to
evaluate success.

Score (1–10): ____

REAFFIRM THE PRIORITY:
KEEP CUSTOMER EXPERIENCE FRONT AND CENTER.

Criteria:

Have regular internal communications that emphasize the importance of customer experience.

Get visible commitment from top leadership on the priority of
customer experience.

Link incentives and rewards to customer experience outcomes.

Score (1–10): ____

Total Score: ____ / 80

Notes: Use this scorecard periodically to assess and improve your leadership's customer centricity. Adjust criteria and weightage as necessary for your organization's specific needs and objectives.

TRAILBLAZING LEADER (70–80 POINTS)

Description: These leaders consistently demonstrate exceptional customer-centric behavior. They prioritize both their employees' and customers' experiences and are proactive in anticipating market changes. Their strategies are both innovative and effective, and they have a clear vision for the future of their organization in the context of customer experience.

PROGRESSIVE LEADER (55–69 POINTS)

Description: These leaders have a strong customer-centric focus but may have a few areas where they could improve. They are open to feedback, and while they have made significant strides in prioritizing customer experience, there's still room for growth.

EMERGING LEADER (40–54 POINTS)

Description: These leaders recognize the importance of a customer-centric approach but may be in the early stages of truly integrating it into their leadership style. They might have a strategy in place but may face challenges in consistent execution or foreseeing long-term implications.

REACTIVE LEADER (25–39 POINTS)

Description: These leaders tend to react to customer feedback rather than proactively shaping experiences. They understand the basics of customer centricity but may prioritize other aspects of their business over customer experience. They might be more focused on short-term gains rather than building lasting customer relationships.

TRADITIONAL LEADER (10–24 POINTS)

Description: These leaders might still be relying heavily on older, conventional methods of business, putting less emphasis on the modern-day importance of customer experience. They might be more product centric or operationally driven, lacking consistent efforts in building and measuring customer-centric strategies.

NOVICE LEADER (0–9 POINTS)

Description: These leaders are at the beginning of their journey toward understanding and integrating customer centricity.

There's significant room for growth, and they might benefit from training, mentorship, and resources to evolve their leadership approach.

It's worth noting that no matter where a leader falls on this spectrum, there's always an opportunity for growth and development. Regularly revisiting the scorecard can help leaders recognize areas of improvement and chart their progress over time.

1. TRAILBLAZING LEADER (70–80 POINTS)

Action items:

Mentorship: Take on mentoring roles to uplift other leaders within the organization.

Thought Leadership: Share insights and learnings at industry conferences or through publications.

Innovation Lab: Create an innovation hub within the company to continually test and improve customer experiences.

Expand Feedback Channels: Seek feedback from a broader audience, such as partners or industry peers.

2. PROGRESSIVE LEADER (55–69 POINTS)

Action items:

Refine Strategy: Regularly review and refine the customer experience strategy for better alignment.

Cross-Functional Collaboration: Engage more departments in customer-centric initiatives.

Advanced Training: Invest in advanced customer-centric leadership training.

Feedback Loop: Establish a more frequent and comprehensive customer feedback loop.

3. EMERGING LEADER (40–54 POINTS)

Action items:

Training: Undergo customer-centric leadership training programs.

Strategy Implementation: Ensure that there's a clear road map for executing the customer experience strategy.

Employee Engagement: Initiate programs that help employees understand and adopt a customer-centric mindset.

Metrics: Start tracking a broader set of KPIs related to customer satisfaction and experience.

4. REACTIVE LEADER (25–39 POINTS)

Action items:

Feedback Systems: Implement more robust customer feedback systems.

Customer-Journey Mapping: Understand customer touchpoints and areas of potential improvement.

Proactive Approach: Shift from a reactive stance to a proactive one by anticipating customer needs.

Employee Training: Conduct basic customer experience and service training for employees.

5. TRADITIONAL LEADER (10–24 POINTS)

Action items:

Research: Dive into modern customer-centric approaches and their benefits.

Customer-Centric Workshops: Attend workshops or seminars focused on customer centricity.

Adopt Tech Tools: Implement tools or platforms that aid in improving customer experience.

Collaboration: Foster collaboration between departments to break silos and adopt a unified customer focus.

6. NOVICE LEADER (0–9 POINTS)

Action items:

Education: Start with basics—books, webinars, and courses on the importance of customer centricity.

Feedback Collection: Begin collecting feedback from customers on their experiences.

Consultation: Seek advice from customer experience experts or consultants.

Vision Setting: Define what customer centricity means for the organization, and set a vision for its importance.

For each leader, a combination of self-awareness, continuous learning, and action can foster growth and a stronger focus on customer centricity.

Notes

CHAPTER 1

1. Ascendo AI, "The World of AI and Chief Customer Officer," LinkedIn, June 28, 2022, https://www.linkedin.com/pulse/world-ai-chief-customer-officer-ascendoai/.

2. "Gartner Says Nearly 90% of Organizations Now Have a Chief Experience Officer or Chief Customer Officer or Equivalents," Press release, February 10, 2020, https://www.gartner.com/en/newsroom/press-releases/2020-02-10-gartner-says-nearly-90--of-organizations-now-have-a-c.

3. Tom Murphy and Haleluya Hadero, "Amazon Will Start Testing Drones That Will Drop Prescriptions on Your Doorstep, Literally," Associated Press, updated October 18, 2023, https://apnews.com/article/amazon-drones-prescription-deliveries-e258b418f2806098de1fba170 69b9fe4.

4. *Harvard Business Review* Analytics Service, *Making Customer Experience the Heart of the Enterprise* (Harvard Business School Publishing, 2021), https://hbr.org/resources/pdfs/comm/salesforce/CXHeartofthe Enterprise.pdf.

5. Neil Davey, "Do These Shocking Stats Prove CEOs Must Have Ownership of CX?" MyCustomer, April 30, 2020, https://www.destinationcrm.com/Articles/Columns-Departments/Customer-Experience/2023-A-Year-of-Reckoning-for-CX-Programs-156693.aspx.

6. The Economist Intelligence Unit, *The Value of Experience: How the C-Suite Values Customer Experience in the Digital Age* (The Economist Intelligence Unit Ltd., 2015), https://impact.econ-asia.com/perspectives/sites/default/files/Genesys_Executive_Summary_-_GLOBAL_FINAL.pdf.

7. Diogo Gonçalves-Candeias, Maria José Chambel, and Vânia Sofia Carvalho, "Is Stress in Contact Centers Inevitable?," *International Journal of*

Environmental Research and Public Health 18, no. 6:2999 (March 2021), https://doi.org/10.3390/ijerph18062999.

8. Denise Lee Yohn, "Engaged Employees Create Better Customer Experiences," *Harvard Business Review*, April 5, 2023, https://hbr.org/2023/04/engaged-employees-create-better-customer-experiences.

9. Michael E. Porter and Nitin Nohria, "How CEOs Manage Time," *Harvard Business Review*, July–August 2018, https://hbr.org/2018/07/how-ceos-manage-time.

10. Connor Brooke, "What's Old Is New Again: 3 Examples of Companies Being Customer-Centric," Business 2 Community, June 26, 2015, https://www.business2community.com/customer-experience/whats-old-is-new-again-3-examples-of-companies-being-customer-centric-01259185.

11. Jeff Fromm, "Gen-Z Is Impacting Customer Experience: Forrester, Gartner, Experience Dynamic Execs Share Insights," *Forbes*, March 16, 2023, https://www.forbes.com/sites/jefffromm/2023/03/16/gen-z-is-impacting-customer-experience-forrester-gartner-experience-dynamic-execs-share-insights/?sh=2a4b50ef7d38.

12. Bruce Temkin, Moira Dorsey, and David Segall, *The Global State of XM, 2020: Survey of 1,292 Executives from Australia, Canada, France, Germany, Japan, Singapore, U.K. and U.S.* (Qualtrics XM Institute, 2020), https://www.qualtrics.com/m/assets/wp-content/uploads/2020/04/XMI_GlobalStateOfXM-2020.pdf.

CHAPTER 2

1. "Delta Is Returning to the Gate to Tweak Unpopular Changes in Its Frequent-Flyer Program," Associated Press, updated September 28, 2023, https://apnews.com/article/delta-loyalty-program-frequent-flyers-24d9620b38fd6493e6b85d52b95bf7f1.

2. Anthony C. Klotz and Mark C. Bolino, "When Quiet Quitting Is Worse Than the Real Thing," *Harvard Business Review*, September 15, 2022, https://hbr.org/2022/09/when-quiet-quitting-is-worse-than-the-real-thing.

3. Qualtrics, "Customer Experience Leaders Had Stronger Stock Returns in 2020 Recession," Press release, July 12, 2022, https://www.qualtrics.com/news/customer-experience-leaders-had-stronger-stock-returns-in-2020-recession/.

4. Ramishah Maruf, "Frontier Airlines No Longer Has a Customer Service Phone Line," CNN, November 26, 2022, https://www.cnn.com/2022/11/26/business/frontier-airlines-customer-service-call-center.

5. Rick Parrish, "2023: A Year of Reckoning for CX Programs," destinationCRM, January 17, 2023, https://www.destinationcrm.com

/Articles/Columns-Departments/Customer-Experience/2023-A-Year
-of-Reckoning-for-CX-Programs-156693.aspx.

6. *HubSpot Annual State of Service in 2022* (HubSpot, 2022), https://
www.hubspot.com/hubfs/assets/flywheel%20campaigns/HubSpot%20
Annual%20State%20of%20Service%20Report%20-%202022.pdf.

7. The Trade Group, "Over 78% of Millennials Prefer Experiences over
Products," LinkedIn, July 13, 2023, https://www.linkedin.com/pulse
/over-78-millennials-prefer-experiences-products-the-trade-group/.

8. Isabella Villani, *Transform Customer Experience: How to Achieve Customer
Success and Create Exceptional CX* (Milton, Australia: John Wiley & Sons
Australia, Ltd, 2019).

9. "86 Percent of Consumers Will Leave a Brand They Trusted After
Only Two Poor Customer Experiences," Press release, Business Wire,
February 2, 2022, https://www.businesswire.com/news/home/20220
202005525/en/86-Percent-of-Consumers-Will-Leave-a-Brand-They
-Trusted-After-Only-Two-Poor-Customer-Experiences.

10. Ani Petrosyan, "Cyber Crime: Number of Compromises and Impacted
Individuals in U.S. 2005–2022," Statista, August 29, 2023, https://www
.statista.com/statistics/273550/data-breaches-recorded-in-the-united
-states-by-number-of-breaches-and-records-exposed/.

CHAPTER 3

1. *Global Leadership Forecast 2023* (Development Dimensions International, Inc. [DDI], 2023), https://media.ddiworld.com/research
/glf2023.pdf.

2. *Wealth Management Digitalization Changes Client Advisory More Than
Ever Before* (Deloitte, 2017), https://www2.deloitte.com/content/dam
/Deloitte/de/Documents/WM%20Digitalisierung.pdf.

3. "Empathy as a Cornerstone of Customer Experience Webinar
(Text)," *Harvard Business Review*, October 29, 2021, https://hbr.org
/sponsored/2021/10/empathy-as-a-cornerstone-of-customer-experience
-webinar.

4. John Doerr, "Why Adobe Killed Performance Reviews," What Matters,
November 26, 2018, https://www.whatmatters.com/articles/why-adobe
-killed-performance-reviews.

5. Will Guidara, *Unreasonable Hospitality: The Remarkable Power of Giving
People More Than They Expect* (New York: Optimism Press, 2022), 125,
Kindle.

6. Monitor Deloitte, *The True Value of Customer Experiences* (Deloitte, 2019),
https://www2.deloitte.com/content/dam/Deloitte/us/Documents
/process-and-operations/us-cons-the-true-value-of-customer
-experiences.pdf.

7. Victoria Bough et al., "The Three Building Blocks of Successful Customer-Experience Transformations," McKinsey & Company, October 27, 2020, https://www.mckinsey.com/capabilities/growth -marketing-and-sales/our-insights/the-three-building-blocks-of -successful-customer-experience-transformations.

CHAPTER 4

1. Wikipedia Contributors, "Amazon Web Services," Wikipedia, https:// en.wikipedia.org/wiki/Amazon_Web_Services.
2. Dominic Barton et al., "Where Companies with a Long-Term View Outperform Their Peers," McKinsey & Company, February 8, 2017, https://www.mckinsey.com/featured-insights/long-term-capitalism /where-companies-with-a-long-term-view-outperform-their-peers.
3. Dennis Carey et al., "Why CEOs Should Push Back Against Short-Termism," *Harvard Business Review*, May 31, 2018, https://hbr .org/2018/05/why-ceos-should-push-back-against-short-termism.
4. Carolyn Dewar, Scott Keller, and Vikram Malhotra, *CEO Excellence: The Six Mindsets That Distinguish the Best Leaders from the Rest* (New York: Scribner, 2022).
5. Anne Marie Knott, "The Real Reasons Companies Are So Focused on the Short Term," *Harvard Business Review*, December 13, 2017, https:// hbr.org/2017/12/the-real-reasons-companies-are-so-focused-on-the -short-term.
6. David M. Cote, *Winning Now, Winning Later: How Companies Can Succeed in the Short Term While Investing for the Long Term* (HarperCollins Leadership, 2020).
7. Blake Morgan, "Please Rate Your Agreement with the Following Items: We Invest Significantly to Improve Our Customer Experience," Graph, *Global Leadership Forecast 2023 Pulse Survey* (DDI, 2023), https://ddi .az1.qualtrics.com/results/public/ZGRpLVVSX2RpT2JYSmtHN 3BTYm9Gdio2NDVjZjMzZmI2NWE2YTAwMDhiYTE5Yjk=#/ pages/Page_fb9ec7fa-c327-43c7-bd71-a92acofa57ef.
8. Sophia Bernazzani Barron, "Here's Why Customer Retention Is So Important for ROI, Customer Loyalty, and Growth," *HubSpot* (blog), March 11, 2022, https://blog.hubspot.com/service/customer-retention.
9. Gartner, "Gartner Says Most Customer Experience Programs Are Not Delivering on the Promise of Improving Differentiation and Helping Brands Better Compete," Press release, May 10, 2022, https://www .gartner.com/en/newsroom/press-releases/gartner-says-most-customer -experience-programs-are-not-deliverin.
10. Jeremy Repanich, "More Than 70,000 Restaurants Closed Because of the Pandemic, a New Report Estimates," *Robb Report*, June 27, 2022,

https://robbreport.com/lifestyle/news/how-many-restaurants-closed -pandemic-1234694652/.

11. Felix Salmon, "The Rise and Fall of Peloton," *Axios*, December 14, 2021, https://www.axios.com/2021/12/14/peloton-stock-covid-pandemic.

12. Thomas Barrabi, "Peloton Cancels Planned $400M Ohio Factory in Frantic Cost-Cutting Bid," *New York Post*, February 9, 2022, https:// nypost.com/2022/02/09/peloton-cancels-planned-400m-ohio-factory -in-cost-cutting-bid/.

13. Lauren Thomas, "Peloton Shares Soar After Company Announces $420 Million Deal for Fitness Equipment Maker Precor," CNBC, December 21, 2020, https://www.cnbc.com/2020/12/21/peloton-to-acquire -fitness-equipment-maker-precor-for-420-million.html.

14. Spectrum News Staff, "Peloton CEO Apologizes for Initial Response on Treadmill Recall: 'We Did Make a Mistake,'" *Spectrum News NY1*, May 7, 2021, https://ny1.com/nyc/all-boroughs/news/2021/05/07 /peloton-ceo-treadmill-recall.

15. United States Consumer Product Safety Commission, "CPSC Warns Consumers: Stop Using the Peloton Tread+," Press release, April 17, 2021, https://www.cpsc.gov/Newsroom/News-Releases/2021/CPSC -Warns-Consumers-Stop-Using-the-Peloton-Tread.

16. *The State of Customer Engagement Report 2023* (Twilio, 2023), https:// www.twilio.com/content/dam/twilio-com/global/en/static-pages /state-of-customer-engagement-report-2023/assets/pdfs/Final _SOCER_2023_EN.pdf.

17. Victoria Vouloumanos, "People Are Sharing Famous Companies That Went Bankrupt over Dumb Decisions, and Now I Finally Know What Happened to Circuit City," *BuzzFeed*, September 8, 2021, https://www .buzzfeed.com/victoriavouloumanos/companies-that-bankrupted -themselves.

18. Marc Benioff, "Create Strategic Company Alignment with a V2MOM," *The 360 Blog*, May 1, 2020, https://www.salesforce.com/blog/how-to -create-alignment-within-your-company/.

19. Ron Ashkenas and Peter D. Moore, "Keeping Sight of Your Company's Long-Term Vision," *Harvard Business Review*, April 8, 2022, https:// hbr.org/2022/04/keeping-sight-of-your-companys-long-term-vision.

CHAPTER 5

1. "Salesforce Report: Nearly 90% of Buyers Say Experience a Company Provides Matters as Much as Products or Services," Salesforce, May 10, 2022, https://www.salesforce.com/news/stories/customer-engagement -research/.

2. Wayne W. LaMorte, "What Is Culture?," Boston University School of Public Health, last modified May 3, 2016, https://sphweb.bumc.bu.edu /otlt/mph-modules/PH/CulturalAwareness/CulturalAwareness2.html.

3. Lyn Wildwood, "25 Latest Personalization Statistics and Trends (2023 Edition)," *Blogging Wizard* (blog), updated July 12, 2023, https:// bloggingwizard.com/personalization-statistics/.

4. James Clear, "Continuous Improvement: How It Works and How to Master It," James Clear, n.d., https://jamesclear.com/continuous -improvement.

5. Sitecore, "New Sitecore Report Shows Brands Must Shift from Transactional to Transparent If They Want to Rebuild Customer Loyalty," Press release, May 24, 2022, https://www.sitecore.com/company/newsroom /press-releases/2022/05/us-brand-authenticity-report.

6. Jeffrey Davis, "Is Our Always-On Culture Choking Creativity?" *Psychology Today* (blog), October 1, 2022, https://www.psychologytoday.com /us/blog/tracking-wonder/202210/is-our-always-on-culture-choking -creativity.

7. Business Wire, "KB Home Named to Newsweek's 2023 List of America's Most Trustworthy Companies, for the Second Consecutive Year," Press release, April 3, 2023, https://finance.yahoo.com/news/kb-home -named-newsweek-2023-120000974.html.

8. Blake Morgan, "The Top 5 Industries Most Hated by Customers," *Forbes*, October 16, 2018, https://www.forbes.com/sites/blakemorgan/2018/10/16 /top-5-most-hated-industries-by-customers/?sh=2d367ce89ob5.

9. IMDb, "*The Bear* (TV Series 2022–)," Internet Movie Database, n.d., https://www.imdb.com/title/tt14452776/.

10. Steritech, "The Future of Customer Loyalty and Perfect Brand Experience: Report," Case Study, n.d., https://www.steritech.com/knowledge -center/case-studies/future-of-customer-loyalty-report/.

CHAPTER 6

1. Michael D. Watkins, *The First 90 Days: Proven Strategies for Getting Up to Speed Faster and Smarter*, Updated and Expanded Edition (Boston: Harvard Business Review Press, 2013).

2. Michael D. Watkins, *The First 90 Days*.

CHAPTER 7

1. Alan Murray, "Tomorrow's Capitalist: My Search for the Soul of Business," Talks at Google, June 25, 2022, YouTube video, 41:24, https:// www.youtube.com/watch?v=mY8kA4TBt_Q&t=1s.

2. Alan Murray, "Tomorrow's Capitalist: My Search for the Soul of Business," Next Big Idea Club, May 24, 2022, https://nextbigideaclub.com/magazine/tomorrows-capitalist-search-soul-business-bookbite/33995/.

3. Tony Seba and James Arbib, "We Are Approaching the Fastest, Deepest, Most Consequential Technological Disruption in History," *Fast Company*, October 5, 2020, https://www.fastcompany.com/90559711/we-are-approaching-the-fastest-deepest-most-consequential-technological-disruption-in-history.

4. Fromm, "Gen-Z Is Impacting Customer Experience."

5. Leah Leachman and Don Scheibenreif, "Using Technology to Create a Better Customer Experience," *Harvard Business Review*, March 17, 2023, https://hbr.org/2023/03/using-technology-to-create-a-better-customer-experience.

6. Jason Dorsey and Chris Johnson, *The State of Customer Experience: Understanding the Hidden Drivers and Expectations of Today's Consumers from Generation Z to Baby Boomers* (Experience Dynamic, 2023), https://www.laneterralever.com/hubfs/Experience%20Dynamic%20The%20State%20of%20Customer%20Experience%20in%202023%20Full%20Report.pdf.

7. Amber Jackson, "Grand View Research: AI Market to Hit US$1.8tn by 2030," *AI Magazine*, July 4, 2023, https://aimagazine.com/articles/grand-view-research-ai-market-to-hit-us-1-811-75bn-by-2030.

8. Bryan Hancock, Bill Schaninger, and Lareina Yee, "How Generative AI Could Support—Not Replace—Human Resources," McKinsey & Company, July 10, 2023, https://www.mckinsey.com/capabilities/people-and-organizational-performance/our-insights/the-organization-blog/how-generative-ai-could-support-not-replace-human-resources.

9. Kevin Surace, "The Largest Business Disruption in History," Medium, March 13, 2017, https://kevinsurace.medium.com/the-largest-business-disruption-in-history-5b36af28799f.

10. Chris Vallance, "AI Could Replace Equivalent of 300 Million Jobs—Report," BBC News, March 28, 2023, https://www.bbc.com/news/technology-65102150.

11. Blair Williamson, "Call Center Turnover Rates: How to Boost Agent Retention," *Nextiva* (blog), July 14, 2022, https://www.nextiva.com/blog/call-center-turnover-rates.html.

12. Teleperformance, "Teleperformance Expands Microsoft Partnership to Launch TP GenAI, a Generative AI Platform to Make Enterprises More Efficient and Human-Centric," Press release, June 20, 2023, https://www.prnewswire.com/news-releases/teleperformance-expands-microsoft-partnership-to-launch-tp-genai-a-generative-ai-platform-to-make-enterprises-more-efficient-and-human-centric-301855095.html.

13. Hayden Field, "Nvidia CEO Jensen Huang Says AI Will Be 'Fairly Competitive' with Humans in 5 Years," CNBC, updated November 30, 2023, https://www.cnbc.com/2023/11/29/nvidia-ceo-ai-will-be-fairly -competitive-with-humans-in-5-years.html.

14. Susan Caminiti, "How Walmart Is Using A.I. to Make Shopping Better for Its Millions of Customers," CNBC, March 27, 2023, https://www .cnbc.com/2023/03/27/how-walmart-is-using-ai-to-make-shopping -better.html.

15. Samantha Kelly, "Google Is Using AI to Change How You Shop," CNN, June 14, 2023, https://edition.cnn.com/2023/06/14/tech/google -ai-shopping/index.html.

16. Sophie Smith, "How AI and AR Can Deliver a Powerful Online and Offline Beauty Experience," TheIndustry.beauty, April 13, 2023, https:// theindustry.beauty/how-ai-and-ar-can-deliver-a-powerful-online-and -offline-beauty-experience/.

17. Bill Briggs, "Kroger's Smart Shelves Ditch the Paper, Drop the Lights and Delight the Shoppers," Microsoft, June 25, 2018, https://news .microsoft.com/transform/kroger-smart-shelves-ditch-paper-drop -lights-delight-shoppers/.

18. Avneet Singh, "Generative AI 'Food Coach' That Pairs Food with Your Mood," *Google for Developers* (blog), May 16, 2023, https://developers .googleblog.com/2023/05/generative-ai-recipe-developers.html.

19. Jennifer Stevenson, "The Future of AI/AR in Retail," *Retail Customer Experience* (blog), May 25, 2023, https://www.retailcustomerexperience .com/blogs/the-future-of-aiar-in-retail/.

20. Heather Haddon, "AI Comes to the Drive-Through. Would You Like Human Interaction with That?," *Wall Street Journal*, June 13, 2023, https://www.wsj.com/articles/ai-fast-food-customer-service-a9151e27.

21. Natasha Lomas, "ChatGPT-Maker OpenAI Accused of String of Data Protection Breaches in GDPR Complaint Filed by Privacy Researcher," *TechCrunch*, August 30, 2023, https://techcrunch.com/2023/08/30 /chatgpt-maker-openai-accused-of-string-of-data-protection-breaches -in-gdpr-complaint-filed-by-privacy-researcher/.

22. Mariah Espada, "Apple TV+'s The Beanie Bubble Explores the True Story of the Women Behind the Beanie Baby Fad," *TIME*, July 28, 2023, https://time.com/6299371/the-beanie-bubble-true-story-apple-tv/.

23. Dana Kennedy, "The Dark Side of Ty Warner, the Reclusive Billionaire Behind Beanie Babies," *New York Post*, October 8, 2022, https://nypost .com/2022/10/08/dark-side-of-ty-warner-the-billionaire-behind-beanie -babies/.

24. US Attorney's Office, Northern District of Illinois, "H. Ty Warner Sentenced to Probation After Paying $80 Million in Taxes and Penalties for Tax Evasion on Funds Hidden in Secret Swiss Bank Accounts,"

Press release, updated July 23, 2015, https://www.justice.gov/usao-ndil /pr/h-ty-warner-sentenced-probation-after-paying-80-million-taxes -and-penalties-tax-evasion.

25. Stephanie Osmanski, "How Much Are Your Beanie Babies Really Worth? 41 Most Valuable Tys of All Time," *Parade*, updated July 28, 2023, https://parade.com/1172319/stephanieosmanski/most-valuable -beanie-babies/.

26. Alina Selyukh, "Bed Bath & the Great Beyond: How the Home Goods Giant Went Bankrupt," NPR, April 24, 2023, https://www .npr.org/2023/04/24/1152070914/bed-bath-the-great-beyond-how-the -home-goods-giant-went-bankrupt.

27. Birdeye, "How David's Bridal Creates Exceptional Omnichannel Experiences with Birdeye," Case Study, n.d., https://birdeye.com/resources /case-studies/david-s-bridal/.

28. Gabrielle Fonrouge, "Not Just Shoplifting: Here's Why Companies Say Retail Theft Is Such a Big Deal," CNBC, May 31, 2023, https:// www.cnbc.com/2023/05/31/what-are-retail-shrink-and-organized-retail -crime.html.

29. Gabrielle Fonrouge, "Shrink and Theft Losses Near $1 Billion at Lowe's—Here's How Much They're Costing Other Retailers," CNBC, September 18, 2023, https://www.cnbc.com/2023/09/08/this-is-how -much-money-retailers-are-losing-to-shrink-retail-theft.html.

30. "Target Predicts $1.3B Profit Loss from Theft," *Loss Prevention Magazine*, May 23, 2023, https://losspreventionmedia.com/target-profit-loss -theft/.

31. Dan Walters, "Annual Crime Report Shows Californians' Fear of Increasing Crime Is Justified," *CalMatters*, July 9, 2023, https://calmatters .org/commentary/2023/07/crime-increase-california-fears-justified/.

32. Arielle Feger, "How Gen Z Shops and Buys in 5 Charts," Insider Intelligence, February 21, 2023, https://www.insiderintelligence.com/content /how-gen-z-shops-buys-5-charts.

33. "Gen Z Shopping Habits," Oberlo, 2023, https://www.oberlo.com /statistics/gen-z-shopping-habits.

34. Brian Solis, "Domino's Pizza Serves Up Innovations in Customer Experience (CX) to Drive Business Growth," *Forbes*, August 15, 2018, https://www.forbes.com/sites/briansolis/2018/08/15/dominos-pizza -serves-up-innovations-in-customer-experience-cx-to-drive-business -growth/.

35. Neil Perkin, "Possible Futures," *Medium*, June 23, 2020, https://medium .com/building-the-agile-business/possible-futures-1e91eecdcb08.

36. "David Geffen," Wikipedia, last modified November 30, 2023, https:// en.wikipedia.org/wiki/David_Geffen.

37. Stephanie Chevalier, "D2C E-Commerce Sales in the U.S. 2019–2024," Statista, November 27, 2023, https://www.statista.com/statistics/1109833/usa-d2c-ecommerce-sales/.

38. *2022 Digital-First Customer Experience Report* (NICE, 2022), https://get.nice.com/rs/069-KVM-666/images/0003959_en_digital-first-cx-report.pdf.

39. BI India Bureau, "Do Customers Still Prefer Speaking to a Human, and Not a Chatbot?" *Business Insider India*, June 2, 2022, https://www.businessinsider.in/tech/enterprise/news/why-customers-still-prefer-speaking-to-a-human-not-chatbox/articleshow/91955173.cms.

40. "What Do Your Customers Actually Think About Chatbots?" *Userlike* (blog), December 15, 2022, https://www.userlike.com/en/blog/consumer-chatbot-perceptions.

41. "Autonomous Robot," Wikipedia, last modified November 13, 2023, https://en.wikipedia.org/wiki/Autonomous_robot.

CHAPTER 8

1. Ben Wigert and Ryan Pendell, "6 Trends Leaders Need to Navigate This Year," Gallup, January 31, 2023, https://www.gallup.com/workplace/468173/workplace-findings-leaders-need-navigate-year.aspx.

2. Holly Muscolino, "Employee Experience and Customer Experience—What Is the Connection?" *International Data Corporation (IDC)* (blog), September 17, 2021, https://blogs.idc.com/2021/09/17/employee-experience-and-customer-experience-what-is-the-connection/.

3. "Number of In-N-Out Burger Restaurants in the United States in 2023," ScrapeHero, November 29, 2023, https://www.scrapehero.com/location-reports/In-N-Out%20Burger-USA/.

4. Alex Beggs, "In-N-Out Served 1,424 Burgers at the Vanity Fair Oscar Party," *Vanity Fair*, March 5, 2014, https://www.vanityfair.com/hollywood/2014/03/vf-oscar-party-tequila-and-donuts.

5. Chloe Sorvino, "In-N-Out Billionaire Lynsi Snyder Opens Up About Her Troubled Past and the Burger Chain's Future," *Forbes*, October 10, 2018, https://www.forbes.com/sites/chloesorvino/2018/10/10/exclusive-in-n-out-billionaire-lynsi-snyder-opens-up-about-her-troubled-past-and-the-burger-chains-future/?sh=79462b54b9cd.

6. "Associate Hourly Salaries in California at In-N-Out Burger," Indeed, last updated November 29, 2023, https://www.indeed.com/cmp/In--n--out-Burger/salaries/Associate/California.

7. Sorvino, "In-N-Out Billionaire Opens Up."

8. Marielle Leon, "Advice from 2018 Best Places to Work Winning Companies," *Glassdoor* (blog), December 12, 2017, https://www

.glassdoor.com/employers/blog/advice-2018-best-place-work-winning
-companies/.

9. Market Force Information, "In-N-Out Burger Wins Consumer
Favor in Market Force Information's New Study," Press release,
November 16, 2022, https://www.prnewswire.com/news-releases
/in-n-out-burger-wins-consumer-favor-in-market-force-informations
-new-study-301679727.html.

10. "Mary Kay Ash," Wikipedia, last modified November 30, 2023, https://
en.wikipedia.org/wiki/Mary_Kay_Ash.

11. Joe Coulombe and Patty Civalleri, *Becoming Trader Joe: How I Did
Business My Way and Still Beat the Big Guys* (HarperCollins Leadership,
2021), 16.

12. Coulombe and Civalleri, *Becoming Trader Joe*, 16.

13. Lisa Freedman, "Why You Only Buy Frozen Food at Trader Joe's," The
Kitchn, updated May 1, 2019, https://www.thekitchn.com/trader-joes
-freezer-section-258479.

14. Caitlin O'Kane, "Starbucks' New CEO Plans to Work as a Barista
Once a Month," CBS News, March 23, 2023, https://www.cbsnews
.com/news/starbucks-ceo-laxman-narasimhan-barista-work-in-stores
-once-a-month-letter-investors/.

15. John Corrigan, "DoorDash Requires All Employees to Make Deliver-
ies," HRD America, January 4, 2022, https://www.hcamag.com/us
/specialization/corporate-wellness/doordash-requires-all-employees-to
-make-deliveries/320995.

16. Nikhil Pandey, ed., "Air New Zealand's CEO Greg Foran Serves Water
on Flight, Photo Goes Viral," New Delhi Television (NDTV), updated
December 22, 2022, https://www.ndtv.com/feature/air-new-zealands
-ceo-greg-foran-serves-water-on-flight-photo-goes-viral-3629924.

17. David Novak, "Follow Indra Nooyi's Example: Become a Leader People Are Excited to Follow," CNBC, September 12, 2018, https://www
.cnbc.com/2018/09/12/pepsico-indra-nooyi-be-a-leader-people-want
-to-follow.html.

18. Novak, "Follow Indra Nooyi's Example."

CHAPTER 9

1. Blake Morgan, "Which Do You Use to Track the Return on Investment
(ROI) of Customer Experience?," Graph, *Global Leadership Forecast
2023 Pulse Survey* (DDI, 2023), https://ddi.az1.qualtrics.com/results
/public/ZGRpLVVSX2RpT2JYSmtHN3BTYm9Gdio2NDVjZj
MzZmI2NWE2YTAwMDhiYTE5Yjk=#/pages/Page_fb9ec7fa
-c327-43c7-bd71-a92ac0fa57ef.

CHAPTER 10

1. Pamela N. Danziger, "5 Reasons That Glossier Is So Successful," *Forbes*, November 7, 2018, https://www.forbes.com/sites/pam danziger/2018/11/07/5-keys-to-beauty-brand-glossiers-success/?sh =3d9a19aa417d.

2. "Glossier Marketing: How the Beauty Brand Used Word-of-Mouth to Shake Up the Industry," *Extole* (blog), August 7, 2022, https://www .extole.com/blog/glossier-marketing-how-the-beauty-brand-used -word-of-mouth-to-shake-up-the-industry/.

3. Danziger, "5 Reasons That Glossier Is So Successful."

Acknowledgments

I'd like to thank my amazing husband, Jacob Morgan—we've been through a lot but what a meaningful fourteen years these have been! Thank you for your support, your love, your partnership and loyalty. I am so grateful for our two absolutely incredible kids, who are genuinely happy kids and make being a mom a blessing and a joy. Thanks for still loving mommy even when she's a hot mess and overwhelmed by the demands of motherhood and career.

I'd like to thank my parents, Debra Malschick and Dr. Michael Landau—thank you for your love, for developing my mind when I was a child, and teaching me how to compete, how to fight for the things I care about, and how to keep getting back on the horse no matter how many times I'm thrown off. I still get thrown off the horse but I'll never quit! Thank you for the time you spend loving my kids. To Jacob's parents, Ella Begelfor and David Morgan, who I can always call no matter the ask. Thank you for being so involved with our family—what a gift you are! I also just think you are amazing people and I would be friends with you even if I weren't your daughter-in-law.

I'd like to acknowledge my editor Tim Burgard at HarperCollins Leadership who believes in the work and gives me this platform to bring my ideas to life. Thank you to Jeff Farr at Neuwirth Associates for providing a second set of eyes. A big thank-you to my research partner DDI, and to Stephanie Neal who helped bring this research to light that helped enhance the book.

Thank you to Rachel on my team who has been an invaluable resource and always has a positive attitude.

And thank you for the customer experience community for continuing to support my work and my ideas. Thank you for sharing my content, giving me ideas, and sharing your stories with me so I can share them with others too.

Index

Index

About the Author

Blake Morgan was called "The Queen of CX" by Meta. She is a customer experience futurist and author of three books on customer experience. She was called one of the top forty female keynote speakers by *Real Leaders Magazine*. Blake is the host of *The Modern Customer Podcast* and contributes to *Forbes*. Blake is a guest lecturer at Columbia University and the University of California, San Diego, as well as adjunct faculty at the Rutgers executive education MBA program. She has worked with companies like Coca-Cola, AT&T, and the Federal Reserve Bank. She lives in Southern California with her husband, their two children, and two dogs.